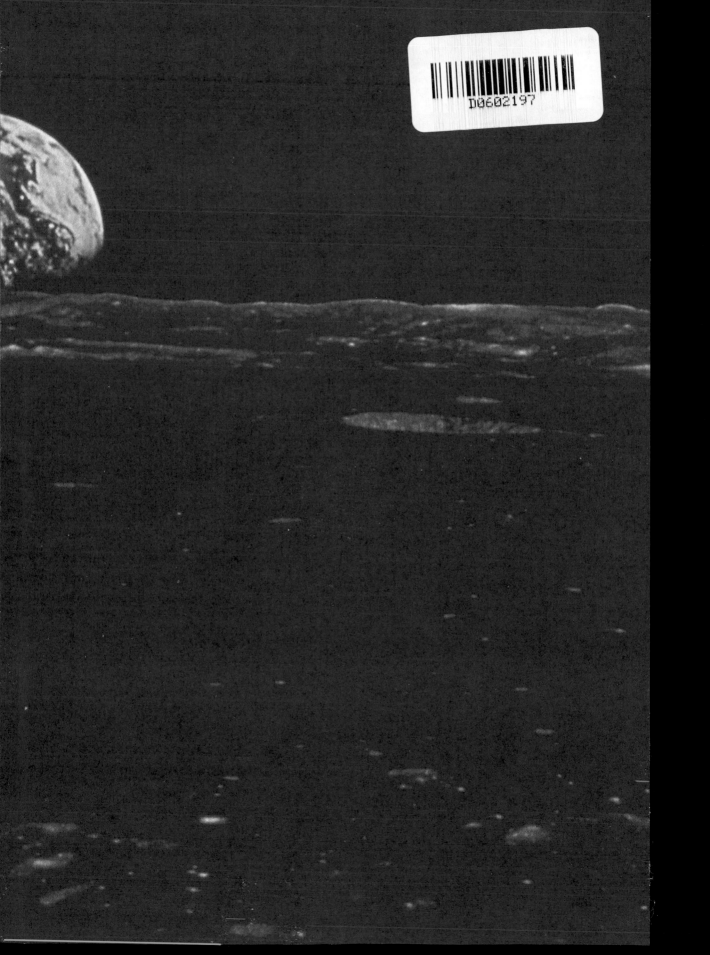

AMERICAN HERITAGE
ILLUSTRATED HISTORY
OF THE UNITED STATES

President Jimmy Carter meets with Egyptian President Anwar Sadat and Israeli Prime Minister Menachem Begin at the close of the Camp David meetings in September, 1978.
THE WHITE HOUSE

FRONT COVER: *A cascade of fireworks climaxes the celebration of the 100th birthday of the Statue of Liberty, the worldwide symbol of freedom, at the entrance to the New York harbor in 1986.*
NEW YORK CITY CONVENTION BUREAU

FRONT ENDSHEET: *The earth, as seen from the moon 240,000 miles away, was photographed by the* Apollo XI *astronauts.*
NASA

CONTENTS PAGE: *President Gerald Ford meets with Soviet leader Leonid Brezhnev at the American Embassy in Helsinki, Finland, at the time of the Helsinki Accords in August, 1975.*
GERALD R. FORD LIBRARY

BACK ENDSHEET: *Cherry trees blossom near the Capitol Building in Washington, D.C.*
HERBERT LANKS, BLACK STAR

BACK COVER: *The Space Shuttle* Challenger *(top left) lifts off moments before it exploded over Cape Kennedy, Florida, in 1986; First Lady Nancy Reagan (top right) admires a panda cub at the Beijing Zoo during a Presidential visit to China in May, 1984; President Ronald W. Reagan meets with Soviet Premier Mikhail Gorbachev in late 1987 (bottom) to discuss bilateral nuclear disarmament.*
XINHUA NEWS AGENCY; NASA; THE WHITE HOUSE

AMERICAN HERITAGE
ILLUSTRATED HISTORY
OF THE UNITED STATES

VOLUME 18

AMERICA TODAY

BY MEDIA PROJECTS INCORPORATED

Created in Association with the
Editors of AMERICAN HERITAGE

CHOICE PUBLISHING, INC.
New York

Library of Congress Catalog Card Number: 87-73399
ISBN 0-945260-18-0
ISBN 0-945260-00-8

This 1988 edition is published and distributed by Choice Publishing, Inc., 53 Watermill Lane, Great Neck, NY 11021
by arrangement with American Heritage, a division of Forbes, Inc.

Manufactured in the United States of America
10 9 8 7 6 5 4 3

CONTENTS OF THE COMPLETE SERIES

Editor's Note to the Revised Edition
Introduction by ALLAN NEVINS
Main text by MEDIA PROJECTS INCORPORATED

EACH VOLUME CONTAINS AN ENCYCLOPEDIC SECTION; MASTER INDEX IN VOLUME 18

CONTENTS OF VOLUME 18

CHAPTER 52

CHANGES IN DOCTRINE AT HOME AND ABROAD

Gerald Ford, the veteran Congressman from Michigan, took office as President at a time of crisis. Already disheartened by the televised carnage of the nation's longest and least popular war, and confused by the social and political upheavals of the last decade, the American people had watched the Nixon Presidency deteriorate into scandal and finally fall apart. In addition, many of the questions raised in the 1960s—questions of economic justice, racial equality, concern for the environment, and, above all, America's role in a rapidly changing world—remained unresolved. It was Ford's task to help heal the nation's wounds and re-unite a people divided on many fundamental issues.

Ford's Presidency was unique in that he was the first American to become chief executive without having been either elected or sworn in upon the death

In 1976, President Ford visited the People's Republic of China, hoping to continue the improvement in Sino-American relations begun by his predecessor, Richard Nixon. Here, he reviews an Honor Guard with Deng Xiaoping.

of his predecessor. His Vice-President, the wealthy former governor of New York, Nelson Rockefeller, was likewise in office as a result of appointment, not election. Ford soon also had the distinction of surviving two assassination attempts, both within the same month, in California.

Barely a month after taking office, Ford granted Richard Nixon a full Presidential pardon for any "federal crimes he committed or may have committed or have taken part in while in office." The Supreme Court later confirmed Ford's right to pardon Nixon, but his action outraged many Americans—after all, he himself had said that the Watergate scandal had proven that no one, not even the President of the United States, was above the law.

Eleven days after pardoning Nixon, Ford took another controversial legal action by offering a limited amnesty to the young men who had resisted the draft or deserted the military during the Vietnam War. Again, Ford's action was met with protest. But Ford was determined to begin healing the deep scars the long,

A fishing boat crammed with Vietnamese refugees is refused permission to land in Thailand. Many thousands of these "boat people" have died fleeing their war-raveraged homeland.

costly Vietnam conflict had inflicted on the United States.

Southeast Asia

Even though American troops had been withdrawn from Vietnam during President Nixon's administration, Southeast Asia and its conflicts remained very much in the public eye. In April, 1975, Americans watched helplessly as the nation's former ally, South Vietnam, was overrun by the troops of Communist North Vietnam. Television news showed heartrending footage of refugees fleeing the wreckage of Saigon in small boats, or clinging to the skids of the last American helicopters to leave the besieged city.

The fall of Saigon marked the end of the American presence in Vietnam. But the presence of Vietnam in America lingered. The sacrifices made by the Vietnam veterans had gone largely unappreciated—not only by the American public but by a Veterans Administration that granted Vietnam veterans substantially fewer benefits than those received by veterans of World War II and Korea. It would be almost a decade before these men and women received the recognition they deserved. The highly-criticized military draft had ended, but despite President Ford's amnesty program many young men who had evaded the draft remained in exile.

Thousands of Vietnamese fled the

forced reunification of their country, and many of those fortunate enough to survive perilous small-boat voyages and overcrowded refugee camps ultimately settled in America. Meanwhile, reports persisted into the 1980s that at least a few American servicemen were still being held captive by the Vietnamese.

In May, 1975, in the aftermath of the Communist victory in Vietnam, troops of the Communist Khmer Rouge in neighboring Cambodia seized an American freighter, the *Mayaguez*, and took its 39-member crew hostage. Ford ordered a rescue mission by the Navy and Marines. It was a costly success—the Cambodians released the hostages, but 38 men of the rescue force were killed. The incident worsened America's already tense relations with Thailand, the country from which the mission was launched, and by the end of 1976, all American forces in Thailand had been withdrawn.

A growing recession

At home, Ford was vexed by the sagging economy he inherited from Richard Nixon. A sharp rise in unemployment had led to the worst full-scale recession since the 1930s. In addition, spending on social programs and the war effort in Vietnam had led to a marked increase in the national deficit, and climbing inflation was rapidly elevating the cost of living for the average American. In his second State of the Union address, on January 19, 1976, President Ford called for "common sense" and a "new realism" in tackling the nation's economic problems. His plan called for a policy of "fiscal restraint" to curb inflation, a reduction in the income tax to promote consumer spending, and a budget designed to reduce the federal deficit.

For all his intimate knowledge of Congress's inner workings, (he had

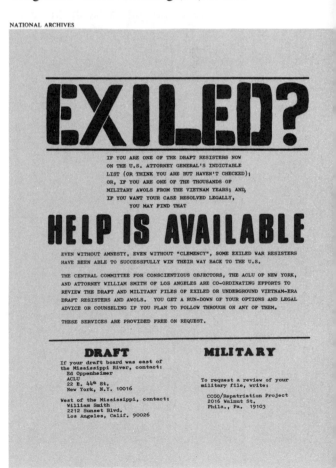

As this poster indicates, thousands of young American men broke the law by refusing to comply with the draft during the Vietnam War. Some went to jail; others fled to Europe or Canada.

served twelve terms as a Congressman from Michigan), Ford, a Republican, had great difficulty in gaining support for his economic policies in a legislature dominated by Democrats. Many of his 66 vetoes (a record number) were overridden as Congress appropriated billions of dollars for health services, welfare, and other social programs. The country drifted deeper into debt. By November 1976 the unemployment rate stood at nearly 8%, with both wholesale and retail prices up and the cost of living rising accordingly.

The federal government was not the only public institution with financial problems in the mid-1970s. By 1975, the nation's largest metropolis, New York City, was on the verge of bankruptcy. President Ford at first refused to support the idea of any federal loan to New York; he eventually relented, and Congress passed legislation authorizing short-term financial aid to the troubled city. In June of 1975, New York City set up a Municipal Assistance Corporation to rebuild the city's finances.

Civil rights under Ford

Building on the achievements of the Civil Rights movement in the 1960s and early 1970s, America's minorities grew increasingly vocal in demanding an end to all forms of inequality. Despite a Supreme Court ruling in support of court-ordered busing of students to achieve racially integrated schools, some communities resisted—most notably Boston, which erupted into racial violence over the issue.

Advocates of women's rights, who had cheered when Congress passed the Equal Rights Amendment in 1972, launched a campaign to have the amendment ratified. By the end of 1975, however, only 34 of the 38 states necessary for ratification had voted in favor of the amendment, and hope faded for its pas-

Despite ratification by a majority of state assemblies, the proposed Equal Rights Amendment fell short of the approval by 38 states required to bring it into law. The pro-ERA campaign was spearheaded by the National Organization for Women, which published this poster.

sage into law. Still, the 1970s saw women entering a variety of trades and professions long limited by law or custom to men, such as police and fire work. Other groups, most notably homosexuals, also fought to end public prejudice and discrimination in jobs and housing.

"Shuttle diplomacy"

Henry Kissinger, Nixon's Secretary of State, stayed on under Ford, and having used "shuttle diplomacy" to help end the Vietnam War, he now applied it to the troubled Middle East. The conflicts between Israel and the Arab nations, as well as disputes within the Arab community itself, were exploding into violence. In 1976, civil war in Lebanon claimed the lives of the American Ambassador and his economic counselor. A growing rapport with Egypt raised hopes for improved Arab-American relations—despite the firm support of Israel by the United States government.

A major feature of Kissinger's foreign policy was "detente," a deliberate reduction of tension between the United States and the Soviet Union without major changes in the two nations' basic positions. This policy made progress possible in the struggle to reduce the threat of nuclear war. At a meeting in Vladivostok, U.S.S.R., in November, 1976, President Ford and Leonid Brezhnev of the Soviet Union agreed to limit the numbers of nuclear missiles, strategic bomber forces, and submarine-launched atomic weapons. Ford later met with Brezhnev, in Moscow, and signed a treaty limiting the size of underground nuclear explosions. Ford also spent five days in China and had a two-hour meeting with Chinese leader Mao Tse-tung. After visits to Indonesia and the Philippines, the President proclaimed what he called the "Pacific Doctrine"—a commitment to "new opportunities for peace without illusion" in that region.

The space program

Space exploration continued to capture America's imagination. Two unmanned Viking spacecraft probes were launched in 1975, and a year later they touched down on the surface of Mars, transmitting stunning photographs and priceless scientific data back to earth. In the summer of 1975, President Ford's policy of detente with the Soviet Union was extended into outer space with the joint U.S.-Soviet Apollo/Soyuz Test Project. On July 17th, an American *Apollo* spacecraft linked up with a Soviet spacecraft, while the two crews conducted a series of joint experiments. Both craft returned safely to earth.

The Bicentennial

The highlight of Ford's Presidency, and perhaps the high point of the entire decade, was the Bicentennial—the year-long celebration of the two-hundredth anniversary of the signing of the Declaration of Independence. For all the trauma of Vietnam, for all the shock of Watergate, for all the disappointments, confusion, and setbacks of recent years, Democracy had survived in America.

After 200 years of often bitter controversy and sometimes violent conflict, the vision of the founding fathers and the principle that "all men are created equal" still served as a touchstone for the American nation.

On July 4, 1976, the President stood in Independence Hall in Philadelphia and proclaimed, "liberty is a living flame to be fed, not dead ashes to be revered." In New York City sailing ships of another era, representing countries from around the world, paraded majestically up the harbor; while in the small towns and villages around the nation, Americans celebrated with concerts, parades, and fireworks.

The election of 1976

It was fitting that the United States entered its third century in an election year. The Presidential campaign of 1976 proved one of the longest and costliest in American history. Public funding of campaigns, approved by the Supreme Court, virtually doubled the candidates' coffers, and much of this money went to buy televison airtime. With its great ability to show the contenders in a wide variety of colorful and dynamic situations—and its tendency to simplify complex issues—television was playing an increasingly influential role in American politics.

The incumbent President Ford's principal rival for the Republican nomination was Ronald W. Reagan, a former motion-picture actor and Governor of California, who had gained prominence in conservative Republican circles dur-

ing Senator Barry Goldwater's unsuccessful bid for the Presidency in 1964. Ford, espousing a more moderate platform, narrowly won the nomination. To appease the conservative faction of the party, he passed over Rockefeller and chose Kansas Senator Robert Dole as his Vice-Presidential running mate.

Several Democratic hopefuls entered the race, their chances brightened by the Republicans' lingering association with the Watergate scandal. Out of the crowded Democratic field, which at one point included California Governor Jerry Brown, former Vice-President Hubert Humphrey, Congressman Morris Udall, and Senator Edmund Muskie, emerged a surprising leading contender for the nomination: a peanut farmer and former Governor of Georgia, Jimmy Carter. Carter had been making a determined effort to build a national reputation since 1973 but was still little known to the nation as a whole. He pictured himself as an "outsider," distancing himself as much as possible from the Washington political scene. His unexpected success in the Democratic primaries propelled him to the nomination. Minnesota Senator Walter Mondale joined the ticket as the Vice-Presidential candidate.

National attention during the ensuing campaign focused on three televised debates between Carter and Ford, under the auspices of the League of Women Voters. Ford, who initially lagged behind Carter in the polls, gained ground after their first debate in Philadelphia. Carter, however, emerged from the debates the front-runner, having turned his

On January 20, 1977, the new President waves to the crowds walking with Rosalynn and their daughter Amy from the Capitol to the White House as part of his "people's inaugural."

biggest weakness—lack of experience in national affairs—into a strength; he convinced many voters that he would bring a fresh, uncorrupted point of view to the White House. Observers predicted a close race, and they were right. When the ballots were counted, Carter had won 50% of the popular vote to Ford's 48%. The electoral percentages were similar, but perhaps the most important statistic of the 1976 election was that only 53% of those eligible had voted.

Having promised to throw off the trappings of Nixon's "imperial presidency," Carter began by proclaiming a "people's inaugural." In his brief address, given on a bright but cold winter day, Carter thanked an obviously moved Gerald Ford for "all he has done to heal our land," and called for "fresh faith in the old dream." Wearing a simple business suit, the new President walked hand-in-hand with his wife Rosalyn and daughter Amy down crowd-lined Pennsylvania Avenue from the Capitol to the White House, where he would soon confront a variety of seemingly intractable problems—both domestic and foreign.

The energy crisis

By the late 1970s America had become more dependent than ever on imported oil, much of it produced in the unstable Middle East, a region always susceptible to political upheavals that might slow or stop the export of petroleum. In 1960, a number of oil-producing Middle Eastern and Latin American nations had formed a cartel (the Organization of Petroleum Exporting Countries, or OPEC) to set prices. The steep rise in foreign oil prices in the 1970s, which OPEC helped to engineer, contributed to the continued growth of American inflation, and Carter and his administration were determined that a full-scale energy crisis—like the one that had plagued the nation during the Arab oil embargo in 1973-74—would be averted. In the spring of 1977, Carter outlined detailed plans for conserving energy, developing alternate sources of energy, and reducing dependence on imported oil. The package that Congress finally adopted in October differed substantially from Carter's specific proposals, but he characterized it as "an important beginning."

Each potential alternative source of energy posed its own problems, however. Nuclear energy, once hailed as the ultimate replacement for fossil fuels such as oil and coal, was opposed by many who felt that its danger, in case of accidents, outweighed its advantages. A serious accident at a nuclear power plant on Three Mile Island, Pennsylvania, in 1979, added fuel to the anti-nuclear cause. Carter said that shutting down all nuclear plants was "out of the question," but he vetoed an eighty million dollar appropriation for a nuclear reactor in Tennessee and pledged to encourage other, less risky energy sources.

When, in July, 1979, the energy crisis still showed few signs of abating, Carter called a "domestic summit." He went into seclusion with 130 prominent Americans for ten days in an attempt to produce a plan that would halt "an erosion of confidence in the future that is threatening the very fabric of America." The result was a six-point proposal that, among other things, called for a tax on excessive profits by oil companies and the development of new energy sources. Congress approved some of the provisions a year later, but a key element—a fee on imported oil—was rejected. Eventually, internal squabbling would lessen OPEC's effectiveness as a cartel and drive down the cost of oil.

Meanwhile, lingering problems from the recession of 1974-75 presented the Carter administration with serious economic troubles: production was falling, and unemployment, inflation, and the federal deficit were all on the rise. Economists were calling the resulting situation "stagflation." To revive the economy, Carter proposed wage and price controls; to reduce unemployment, he urged creation of New Deal-style public-works projects. But all his proposals either were drastically scaled back

ESTADOS UNIDOS   SECRETARIO GENERAL   PANAMA

In 1978, after protracted negotiations with both the Panamanian government and American lawmakers, President Jimmy Carter signed an agreement with Panamanian President Omar Torrijos Herara which will ultimately cede ownership of the Panama Canal to Panama, and guarantee the Canal Zone's neutrality.

by Congress or bogged down completely.

Foreign policy and arms control

Carter had announced in his inaugural address that the U.S. ". . . will not seek to dominate or dictate to others." Shortly after taking office he reinforced this message with cables to all nations asking for a "world order more responsive to human aspirations." Aided by Secretary of State Cyrus Vance and U.S. Ambassador to the United Nations Andrew Young, the Carter Administration began to shape a foreign policy based on a firm insistence that human rights be protected worldwide. The United States cut off aid to nations such as Brazil and Argentina which, although friendly to U.S. interests, practiced political repression of their citizens.

The most controversial foreign- policy decision of the Carter years concerned the Panama Canal. Early in the Carter administration the United States and Panama agreed on conditions for returning control of the Panama Canal Zone to the nation of Panama in the year 2000. Carter and the President of Panama signed the two-part treaty, and it was subsequently ratified by a plebiscite in Panama and approved by the Senate Foreign Relations Committee. A bitter debate over the treaty then engulfed the Senate for four months. Conservative Republican senators charged that the Canal was not only vital to American commerce but was an important strategic link in the U.S. defense network. If the Canal were to fall into unfriendly hands,

they argued, U.S. vessels would have to make a lengthy detour around the tip of South America to move between the Atlantic and Pacific oceans. Supporters of the treaty argued that returning the canal to Panama would be perceived by Central American leaders as a goodwill gesture and thus gain support for America in that strategic and unstable region. The Senate finally ratified the treaty by the required two-thirds vote in April. A formal ceremony marked the treaty's acceptance in Panama City on June 16, 1978.

Seeking to promote goodwill between America and the Third World, Carter made a tour of some 16,000 miles in January 1978 and traveled to Africa and South America the following April. His attention, however, was being drawn increasingly to the embattled Middle East. America's strongest ally in the region, Israel, had long been in conflict with its predominantly Arab neighbors, especially Lebanon, where large numbers of Palestinians had been left without a homeland since the creation of the state of Israel in 1948. In 1978, Carter urged Israel's Prime Minister, Menachem Begin, to seek a settlement of his country's differences with Egypt. Anwar Sadat, Egypt's president, visited Israel despite denunciations by the heads of other Arab nations, and after a year of sporadic negotiations, the two leaders hammered out the terms of an agreement, at Camp David, the presidential retreat in Maryland. The Camp David accords established peace between two nations with a long history of enmity, and Begin and

Sadat received a joint Nobel Peace Prize for their efforts. The accords, signed under the auspices of the United States and at the urging of President Carter, marked a significant victory for U.S. foreign policy. The hope for wider peace in the Middle East was dimmed, however, when President Sadat was assassinated in 1981.

The late 1970s saw Americans becoming increasingly concerned over the proliferation of nuclear weapons. On May 6, 1979, an anti-nuclear demonstration in Washington—against nuclear energy as well as nuclear weapons—drew 65,000 protesters; other demonstrations took place around the nation. Many Americans called for a return to the bargaining table to negotiate an arms-limitation settlement with the Soviet Union.

Relations between the United States and the Soviet Union had cooled since the arms-limitation agreements of 1972, especially after the Carter administration condemned Soviet and Cuban intervention in Africa and spoke out in support of Soviet dissidents. Nevertheless, Carter and Soviet leader Leonid Brezhnev met in Vienna in June, 1979, to sign a strategic-arms-limitation pact known as SALT II. On his return to Washington, Carter addressed a joint session of Congress, stating that the agreement was "not a favor we are doing for the Soviet Union" but "a deliberate, calculated move we are making as a matter of self-interest—a move that happens to serve the goals of both security and survival, that strengthens both the military position of the United States and the cause of world peace." However, the Senate was never able to muster the votes necessary to ratify SALT II.

The possibility of further arms talks with the Soviet Union faded when the U.S.S.R. invaded Afghanistan in 1979. In December of that year Soviet troops entered the capital city of Kabul, ostensibly at the request of Afghanistan's leaders, and put the nation under military occupation. Carter joined the United Nations in protesting the Soviet action and ordered a grain embargo against the U.S.S.R. He also called for a boycott of the 1980 Moscow Olympic games.

At home, Carter sought to strengthen the nation's defenses without adding to its nuclear stockpile. In 1980, he vetoed a defense bill which called for the construction of a nuclear-powered super aircraft carrier, but he approved plans for smaller carriers. He opposed the development and deployment of the controversial B-1 bomber, arguing that it was far too expensive ($100,000,000 per plane) and not essential to the nation's defense. However, he did support production of the nuclear-warhead-carrying MX missile system. Debate over the MX missile would continue into the Reagan presidency.

In 1978, Congress, in accord with Carter's human-rights policy, cut off aid to the corrupt dictatorship of Anastasio Somoza in Nicaragua. At the same time, a rebel movement aimed at toppling the Somoza government, which had held sway over Nicaragua for 46 years, was gaining momentum. After seven weeks of intense civil war in the summer of 1979, the rebels—known as Sandinistas, after a 1930s Nicaraguan revolutionary, Augusto Sandino—defeated the National Guard, forced Somoza to flee the country, and seized power. The United States immediately recognized the new Sandinista government, but opposition to it soon arose among conservative Americans, as its Marxist leanings and ties with the Soviet Union became apparent. A guerrilla war erupted between the Sandinistas and a coalition of their opponents, the "Contras," which included some remnants of the Somoza forces. American public opinion became sharply divided between those favoring a non-interventionist policy and others, including Presidential-hopeful Ronald Reagan, who wanted to prevent any Communist presence in a region close to the United States.

Refugees

The United States once again became the promised land for large numbers of refugees in the 1970s. The fall of Vietnam produced hundreds of thousands of "boat people"—Vietnamese who fled their homeland, unwilling to live under Communism or fearing reprisals from the new regime. President Carter used his executive authority to expand immigration quotas and allow large numbers of Vietnamese to settle in America, and he answered criticism of this policy by stating, "We are a country of refugees."

The thorniest refugee problem, however, was posed by a sudden and unexpected influx of Cubans into the southern United States. Carter's policy of encouraging asylum seekers was sorely tested when the trickle of Cubans allowed out by Fidel Castro swelled to a torrent in 1980.

Thousands of people crowded the port of Mariel, Cuba, and were taken to Florida by a flotilla of private American vessels. Among them were bona fide refugees and political dissidents, but, as soon became clear, Castro was also using the Mariel boatlift as an opportunity to deport mental patients and hardened criminals. By the end of 1980, more than 94,000 Cubans had arrived on our shores. The U.S. government spent $300 million resettling most of them; about 2,500 others were committed to detention centers or mental hospitals because of criminal records or psychiatric histories. Deportation proceedings for these "excludables" began in 1984 under the provisions of an agreement between the United States and Cuba. In 1985, however, Castro suspended the agreement as a protest against U.S. radio broadcasts to Cuba. When the treaty was reactivated in November, 1987, Cuban prisoners, now facing possible deportation back to Cuba, rioted in federal detention centers at Oakdale, Louisiana, and Atlanta, Georgia. Declaring that they would rather die than return to Cuba, the Cubans took control of the facilities and held guards and other personnel hostage. Both sieges ended without fatalities within two weeks when Attorney General Edwin Meese declared a moratorium on deportation of Mariel Cubans and promised an individual review of each

Under an amnesty granted by Fidel Castro in 1980, thousands of refugees fled across the Florida Straits from Cuba to the United States. The Carter administration accepted many as a humanitarian act; unfortunately, some proved to have been hardened criminals flushed from Cuba's jails.

detainee's case by a special panel of the Justice Department.

Civil rights under Carter

The struggle for black civil rights took on a new character in the late 1970s. The sweeping legislation and huge demonstrations of the 1950s and 1960s had given way to a more subdued, but no less determined, effort to attain equality.

Blacks were proving a powerful force in American politics. By the end of the decade blacks had been elected as mayors of a number of American cities, including Newark and Chicago; prominent civil rights activist Andrew Young became the first black appointed as Ambassador to the United Nations; and Patricia Harris became the first black woman cabinet member as President Carter's Secretary of Housing and Urban Development.

Allen Bakke challenged affirmative-action quotas following his rejection from the University of California, Davis, Medical School. Charging "reverse discrimination" Bakke took his case to the Supreme court in 1978

But many people were questioning how well black Americans, on the whole, were faring politically and economically. In 1975, The Civil Rights Commission found that blacks in some areas were still being prevented from voting, despite federal legislation to insure that right. Black unemployment consistently stood at twice the national average. One study reported that 30% of all American blacks lived in poverty—as opposed to 10% of whites.

Programs such as Affirmative Action, which encouraged quotas for black participation in government, business, and education, were sometimes criticized as promoting "reverse discrimination" against whites. In one instance, Allen Bakke, a white California man, was denied admission to the University of California Medical School. Bakke had been passed over to fill a racial quota. He took his case to the Supreme Court, which ruled in Bakke's favor, but did not rule against affirmative action per se.

The environment

The deterioration of the environment and the depletion of natural resources continued to draw national attention. Alarm over the effects of chemical dumping was heightened when hundreds of families were forced to leave their homes on the Love Canal in Niagara Falls, New York, because of contamination of land by illegally buried chemical waste. Carter declared a state of emergency for the area. In general, Carter supported the efforts of environmental activists and conservationists, and he

Islamic fundamentalist followers of the Ayatollah Khomeini burn an American flag during an anti-American demonstration in Iran in 1980. Scenes like this added to American frustration during the Iran hostage crisis.

signed into law an act creating 100 national parks and preservation projects.

The most spectacular environmental event of Carter's Presidency, however, was not man-made but natural. The Mt. St. Helens volcano in southwestern Washington state erupted from mid-May to mid-June 1980, killing at least 28 and devastating a vast tract of land. Damage was estimated at $2.7 billion. Scientists estimated that the force of the blast was 300 times greater than that of the atomic bomb dropped on Hiroshima.

The Iran crisis

An eruption of another kind, in Iran, wrecked the last months of Carter's Presidency and denied him a reasonable chance of winning a second term. Oil-rich Iran, formerly known as Persia, had been ruled since 1941 (except for a brief period of revolt in 1953) by the U.S.-backed Pahlavi dynasty. By the late 1970s large segments of the Iranian population had become dissatisfied with the rule of Shah Mohammad Reza Pahlavi. His most vehement opponents were fanatic religious fundamentalists who reviled his modernization programs and his attempts to encourage western culture in a nation deeply rooted in Moslem tradition. The Shah's often viciously brutal repression of any opposition had turned great numbers of ordinary Iranians against him as well.

In early 1979, the Shah was deposed in a popular revolt and forced to flee the country, and Moslem clergy under the leadership of the Ayatollah Ruhollah Khomeini seized control of the government. They pledged a cutback in oil production and a return to Islamic fundamentalism, but above all, they expressed bitter opposition to America—which Khomeini called the "great Satan." On November 4, 1979, Iranian militants seized the United States Embassy in the capital city of Tehran and took 52 Americans hostage.

The imprisonment of the Americans, a clear violation of universal standards of behavior toward diplomatic personnel, created a groundswell of outrage and frustration in the United States. Despite international protest and the freezing of Iranian assets in the United States, Khomeini not only refused to free the hostages but declined even to negotiate. American anger grew daily as television news programs showed the hostages being paraded through the streets of Tehran by their captors. Despite Khomeini's pledge that any attempt to free the hostages by force would result in their death, Carter came under growing political and public pressure to take more aggressive steps.

In April, 1980, he approved a rescue mission by a specially-trained U.S. Army unit. The hostage-rescue team flew to Iran and landed in a remote desert, planning to stage a raid on Tehran from there. The mission had to be called off when one of the aircraft needed to airlift the hostages to safety malfunctioned. Then, as the force was preparing to withdraw, a transport plane and a helicopter collided and exploded. Eight Americans died in the fiery crash, the hostages remained in captivity, and America's frustration increased. President Carter, almost totally absorbed in the crisis, rapidly lost popularity. It was clear that other candidates in the 1980 Presidential election would profit from his helpless situation.

The election of 1980

Inflation, unemployment, the energy crisis, the hostages in Iran—these were the issues confronting Americans in 1980. Conservative sentiment was growing in reaction to America's domestic troubles and loss of international prestige over the last decade.

Despite a challenge by Senator Edward Kennedy of Massachusetts, President Carter won the Democratic nomination, and he again chose Walter Mondale as his running mate. The Re-

Homosexuals were another minority group to come to the fore during the 1970s in the broadening struggle for civil rights.

publican nomination went to Ronald Reagan, with George Bush—Reagan's closest contender for the Republican nomination—as his Vice-Presidential candidate. Reagan campaigned on a platform advocating reduced taxes, increased military strength, and a decreased role generally for the federal government. And when the polls closed in November, the 51% of the U.S. electorate that voted showed their clearcut support for Reagan's plans. He polled 43,899,248 popular votes to Carter's 36,481,435 and garnered 489 electoral votes to Carter's 49. The United States would enter the 1980s not only with a new president but with a new set of goals.

Americans in recent decades, many activists charged that true racial equality had yet to be achieved. They pointed to the high rate of black unemployment, which throughout the decade consistently ran at least double the national figure for whites. Vernon Jordan, Jr., President of the National Urban League, charged that black Americans were on the "brink of disaster." Black activists were also disappointed by the resignation of Andrew Young, a former associate of Dr. Martin Luther King, Jr., from his post as U.S. Ambassador to the United Nations in June of 1979. Young had stepped down after a storm of criticism over his unauthorized meeting with a representative of the Palestinian Liberation Organization—an organization with which the United States had no official dealings because it committed terrorist acts against Israel.

THE NEW CHINA

XINHUA NEWS AGENCY

In December 1951, when U.S. Marines were slogging through the frozen wastes of Korea's Chosin Reservoir battling thousands of Communist Chinese soldiers, few Americans would have dreamed that in just twenty years the President of the United States and the Premiere of Communist China would toast each other at a banquet in Beijing— or that within thirty years, American tourists would stroll along the parapets of the Great Wall, Chinese and American technicians would work side by side on scores of cooperative projects, and an American student (above) would have a starring role with a Chinese Opera company.

The United States refused to recognize the existence of the People's Republic of China for two decades following the Communist Mao Tse-Tung's victory over the Nationalist forces of Generalissimo Chiang Kai-Shek in 1949, supporting instead the Nationalists, exiled to the offshore island of Taiwan. For twenty years, America and China stood at opposite ends of the ideological, cultural, and geographic worlds. But by the early 1970s, a change was in the wind. Unbeknownst to the world, Secretary of State Henry Kissinger flew to China on a secret diplomatic mission in 1971. Restrictions on commerce and travel were eased. And in 1972, President Nixon traveled to China, and with his visit a new era of friendship and cooperation between the two nations began.

THE NEW CHINA

Some American communities have become "sister cities" to Chinese cities to foster cultural exchanges and trade. Above, Mayor Linda Jobensen of Boulder, Colorado, visits a Buddhist monastery in Boulder's sister city of Lhasa in the Chinese autonomous region of Tibet. Tibet is one of China's most troubled regions. Once an independent nation, it was conquered by mainland China in 1951. As recently as 1987, American tourists were detained for photographing Tibetans protesting China's domination of this ancient, mountainous land.

Cultural exchanges between the U.S. and China often focus on the unique aspects of each nation's culture. Shown top right is a member of Project Troubador, a traveling American entertainment troupe featuring singers, mimes, and other folk performers, with a singer from the world-renowned Beijing Opera.

Americans and Chinese have come together for sporting events since the "ping-pong diplomacy" of the early 1970s. Right, a joint Sino-American drifting team floats down the Tuotuo river on the upper reaches of the Yangtze.

PHOTO BY TANG SHIZENG

PHOTO BY MA QIANLI

This coal mine, in Shanxi province, is a joint venture between China and an American mining company, trying together to tap part of China's vast mineral resources. Below, a team of Chinese and American technicians test soil in Shanxi province to determine the best spot for a coal-processing station.

The revolution in Sino-American relations is but a small part of China's ongoing struggle to modernize and industrialize. Shown above is the first BJ/XJ 213 jeep rolling off the assembly line at Beijing in 1985. The Chinese effort at modernization requires up-to-date transportation, such as this MD-82 jet aircraft, to connect China with the world and span the vast distances within its own borders.

PHOTO BY LI PING

JIMMY CARTER LIBRARY

President Jimmy Carter never visited China while in office, but he did host the first Sino-American talks on U.S. soil in January, 1979. Above, he chats with Deng Xiaoping.

President Reagan hosted Chinese officials in Washington in January, 1983, and in April 1984 traveled to China. The President and Mrs. Reagan are shown here at the tomb of the Emporer Qinshihuang.

CHAPTER 53

THE MARCH OF EVENTS, THE CHALLENGE OF TOMORROW

Though Ronald Reagan was 69 years old when he became President, he took office with a style that seemed fresh, and almost youthfully vigorous. On the very hour of his inauguration, the Iranian militants announced the release of their American hostages after 444 days in captivity. The nation's frustration turned to joy as the freed Americans were flown first to Germany, then back to the United States. Few Presidents have taken office at such a moment of national happiness as Ronald Reagan, and few have come to Washington more determined to set the nation on a conservative course. Reagan and his key people believed that the federal government had become too big, too powerful, bloated by overspending, and dangerously in debt. The President was committed to the idea of a "New Federalism"—the

President Ronald Reagan and First Lady Nancy Reagan. With his affable manner and political optimism, President Reagan sought to inspire a new sense of hope and confidence in America.

idea, put simply, that the less the federal government involved itself in the life of individual citizens, the better it would be for American society as a whole. Under the New Federalism, states and municipalities would assume responsibilities for social programs, taxes would be reduced, and government regulation of many segments of the economy would cease. In theory, these measures would provide a climate in which business would flourish and stimulate the sagging economy. The nation would then recover from the inflation and unemployment of the 1970s. With Republicans dominating the Senate and the Democrats holding only a slim majority in the House, the President had little difficulty in passing substantial tax cuts as the keystone of his program. Reagan's ideas were not without their critics, however. They charged that those highest in the economic hierarchy would reap most of the benefits of the plan. The only real benefits received by lower and middle class Americans would be those that "trickled down"

David Stockman (above) was Director of the Office of Budget and Management during the sweeping economic changes of President Reagan's "New Federalism" in the early 1980s.

from above. And to a great extent the critics were proven right. In 1982, the mid-point of Reagan's first term, the unemployment rate had risen to a post-Depression high of 9.7%. Black unemployment was even higher, and unemployment among black teenagers stood at an alarming 48%.

Farmers, particularly, had severe financial problems. In addition to an already unfavorable market for agricultural products, they had been hard hit by Carter's embargo on grain shipments to the Soviet Union. Reagan lifted the embargo, but the sight of grim farm families watching their land sold at auction was

to be a persistent image throughout the 1980s.

And then, slowly and sporadically, the economy began to improve. Oil prices fell dramatically as the OPEC nations squabbled among themselves. The inflation rate began to drop, and the economic well-being of many Americans brightened.

The dollar and the deficit

America's status as the world's mightiest industrial nation had declined throughout the 1970s, a trend that continued into the Reagan Presidency. The automobile industry, one of the major barometers of the nation's economic health, was grappling with the grim problems of falling sales, rising prices, and intense foreign competition, especially from Japan. Many automobile plants cut back their production drastically or shut down altogether, forcing thousands of workers into unemployment. The federal government granted a multi-billion dollar loan to "bail out" the ailing Chrysler Corporation. The decline in American productivity and an increasing demand for foreign-made goods—which were often less expensive and of higher quality than their American equivalents—produced support for a "new protectionism," including tariffs and other measures, to restrict the flow of imported goods into the United States and protect American jobs. Economists and business analysts also advocated new management techniques and greater labor-management cooperation to return

President Reagan meets with his Economic Council—the men responsible for shaping his economic reforms—including Treasury Secretary James Baker and James Miller, David Stockman's replacement as Director of the Office of Management and Budget.

American industry to the wordwide preeminence it had once held.

The demand for imported goods led to a growing trade imbalance between the United States and other nations. At first, the dollar was high in value compared with foreign currencies, with the inevitable result that lower-priced imports exceeded exports by large amounts. The U.S. trade deficit grew by $112 billion between 1980 and 1985 alone. In 1987, the United States, in cooperation with several other nations, began allowing the dollar to fall in value in relation to other currencies in an effort to reverse the trade imbalance.

The federal deficit was a rapidly growing concern. Lower taxes, coupled with a burgeoning federal budget—especially swollen by Reagan-era increases in defense spending—made for huge increases in the deficit. In 1980, the deficit stood at just over $914 billion; by 1987, it had grown to more than two trillion dollars. After much deliberation Congress passed the Gramm-Rudman-Hollings Act, which, in its final form, mandated an automatic across-the-board $23 billion dollar deficit reduction unless Congress came up with a better specific proposal. Legislators and administrative officials hurriedly agreed to a

GIVE
AMERICA
A FIGHTING
CHANCE.

STOP
UNFAIR
IMPORTS.

IMPORTED

FFACT FIBER, FABRIC &
APPAREL COALITION
FOR TRADE

As inexpensive, high-quality imported goods—from television sets to automobiles—have competed with American products, some labor leaders and politicians have called for a "new protectionism" to preserve American jobs.

$76-billion reduction spread out over two years.

Democrats and Republicans alike agreed that the deficit had to be reduced, but disagreed on which items were to be cut; they were especially troubled by the prospect of cutting long-established programs such as Social Security, usually considered untouchable. Conservatives opposed reductions in defense spending, but by the end of 1987, it seemed that some reductions would have to be made.

Lebanon, Libya, and terrorism

As it had been for Carter, the Middle East remained an relentless source of concern for President Reagan and his foreign policy advisers. In 1982, Israeli military forces invaded the war-torn neighboring nation of Lebanon, to try to drive Palestinian Liberation Organization (PLO) forces from the city of Beirut. After fierce fighting in which hundreds of people, many of them civilians, were killed, the PLO guerrillas were evacuated by sea to the Libyan city of Tripoli.

Israel's invasion of Lebanon drew a storm of international protest, especially when it was learned that Lebanese militiamen had slaughtered more than 600 persons, including women and children, in two Palestinian refugee camps after Israeli guards allowed the militiamen in to search for weapons. Israel began to withdraw its troops in December 1982, but violence between various Lebanese factions led to the landing of a multinational peacekeeping force, including U.S. Marines, to restore order in Beirut. Despite the presence of the force, the fighting continued.

On October 23, 1983, a Mercedes truck crammed with explosives drove into the main Marine compound in Beirut and blew up. Two hundred and forty-one Americans were killed. The terrorist bombing of the Marine barracks

Members of the United Nations peacekeeping force man an outpost in Lebanon. The multinational U.N. force, which arrived in Lebanon in June, 1979, was faced with the nearly impossible task of maintaining order in a nation torn by factional strife.

produced a wave of outrage among Americans and led to a severe questioning of the U.S. role in Lebanon. After presiding over a national service for the slain Marines, President Reagan ordered the surviving Marines to evacuate the city. The last of the American troops withdrew from Beirut in February 1984.

Terrorism around the world increased at a frightening rate in the 1980s. Every day, it seemed, newspaper headlines announced some new act of terrorism abroad. Extremists assassinated Egyptian President Anwar Sadat and Swedish Prime Minister Olaf Palme, and Pope John Paul II was wounded in an assassination attempt in Rome. In October 1985, Palestinian hijackers seized the Italian cruise ship *Achille Lauro* in the Mediterranean Sea, in a bid to force Israel to free 50 Palestinian prisoners. The brutal murder of an American passenger prompted a mission by U.S. Navy fighter jets to intercept and force down in

U.S. Marines landed in Lebanon in 1983 in an effort to quell the bitter fighting in Beirut. Two-hundred and sixty Marines died in Lebanon, most in the terrorist truck bombing of their Beirut headquarters on October 23, 1983.

Sicily a plane carrying the hijackers to safety. This gave America a rare victory in the shadowy struggle against terrorism. In June 1985, a TWA airliner was hijacked on a flight from Athens to Rome and forced to land in Beirut, Lebanon. A U.S. Navy diver on board was killed, and the other passengers and crew were held hostage for 17 days. Twenty people were killed in airport bombings at Rome and Vienna on Christmas Day, 1985, and two U.S. soldiers died in the bombing of a Berlin discotheque. With public concern mounting, President Reagan took an increasingly hard-line stance against terrorism, calling for swift retaliatory actions. The discovery of evidence apparently linking the Berlin bombing with Libya's fanatically anti-American dictator Muammar Qaddafi led to a raid against his country by U.S. warplanes. On April 15, 1986, American aircraft bombed the Libyan cities of Benghazi and Tripoli. Qaddafi survived despite direct hits on his home and headquarters. One U.S. plane, with two crewmen aboard, was lost. The United States had previously tangled with Libya in March, 1986, when Libyan patrol boats fired missiles at U.S. naval forces on maneuvers off the Libyan coast. U.S. ships and aircraft fired back, hitting two Libyan vessels.

Iran, Iraq, and the Persian Gulf

The war that broke out between Iran and Iraq in 1980 grew into a bloody, drawn-out conflict. Despite international efforts at mediation, the war became, by 1987, the fourth largest war in the twen-

Damaged by a missile mistakenly launched by an Iraqi warplane, the U.S.S. Stark *lies dead in the water of the Persian Gulf in May, 1987. Thirty-seven American sailors lost their lives in the mishap.*

tieth century in terms of deaths. Iran mined the Persian Gulf, the source of a significant amount of the world's oil, and attacked the tankers of several nations with rocket and missiles. The United States remained neutral in the Iran-Iraq conflict, but stated that it was committed to freedom of passage for merchant vessels in the international waters of the Gulf. The situation in the Gulf deteriorated further on May 17, 1987, when an Iraqi warplane fired a missile at the frigate U.S.S. *Stark*, killing 37 crewmen. The United States accepted Iraq's explanation that the attack was due to a case of mistaken identity, but the *Stark* tragedy again redoubled tensions in an already volatile region. The United States offered to reflag foreign oil tankers as American vessels and provide U.S. Navy ships to escort them through the Gulf. More U.S. military forces were sent into the area, including minesweepers to clear the waters of Iranian mines, and attack helicopters to intercept Iranian patrol boats. As 1987 came to an end, Iran and Iraq were still at war and oil was still flowing, despite more than 400 attacks on shipping in the Gulf since the conflict began.

On October 25, 1983, U.S. forces invaded the tiny Caribbean island nation of Grenada to safeguard American students during a period of political violence.

Grenada and Central America

On October 25, 1983, U.S. Marines and paratroopers landed on the tiny Caribbean island of Grenada, ostensibly to rescue American medical students from possible harm in a turbulent political situation. After a brief period of combat, the island was captured and the medical school secured. American casualties were 18 dead and 45 wounded; 24 Cubans and 45 Grenadians were killed. President Reagan said the invasion had been carried out in response to a request for American intervention by the Organization of Eastern Carribean States—which was alarmed at Grenada's Marxist government and growing ties with Cuba—as well as out of concern over the medical students' safety.

From the beginning of the Reagan Presidency, a major focus of U.S. concern in Central America was El Salvador, a nation torn by both Communist insurgency and the activities of brutal right-wing groups. Eventually, American aid to El Salvador was cut off; then financial assistance was resumed when Jose Napoleon Duarte became President. The United States also sent a number of military advisers to El Salvador. The civil war continued, and by August, 1981, nearly 300,000 Salvadorians were refugees, many seeking political asylum in the United States.

But it was the Sandinista victory in Nicaragua that would preoccupy the Reagan administration. The President, an implacable foe of the Marxist Sandinistas and a staunch supporter of the anti-Sandinista "Contra" guerrillas, repeatedly voiced his concern over the presence of a Marxist government in a nation relatively close to the American border and in a region important to U.S. interests. He also saw the Sandinista government, which received large amounts of aid from the Soviet Union and other Communist nations, as a tool of "Soviet imperialism" in Central America. The President hailed the Contras as "freedom fighters" and urged a reluctant Congress to appropriate millions of dollars for both military and humanitarian aid to the anti-Sandinista forces.

A majority of Americans, according to most polls, never shared Reagan's enthusiasm for the Contras, particularly as evidence of Contra atrocities and corruption mounted. With memories of the Vietnam War still haunting the nation, protests against U.S. involvement in Nicaragua increased. To mollify public opinion, Reagan announced in April, 1983, that he had "no thought of sending American combat troops to Nicaragua." Many American troops were, however, being sent on training missions to Nicaragua's neighbor, Honduras, and in April, 1984, the Central Intelligence Agency announced that the United States had mined Nicaraguan harbors, damaging eight ships. That admission touched off an international protest and a ruling by the World Court, in 1986, that the United States had violated international law.

Most American leaders favored a diplomatic, rather than military, effort at bringing peace to Nicaragua. Reagan opposed the "Contadora" peace plan proposed by several Central American nations, putting forth instead his own plan, drafted with House Speaker Jim Wright, in August, 1987. The Reagan-Wright plan was set aside when an alternative plan was offered by Oscar Arias Sanchez, President of Costa Rica, in the fall of 1987. Arias' plan was adopted by five Central American nations, and international support for his efforts at promoting peace in the region was heightened when he received the 1987 Nobel Peace Prize.

The election of 1984

By 1984, the economy had stabilized, inflation was moderating, and President Reagan, bolstered by these favorable trends, declared his intention to run for a second term. His 1984 platform was much the same as that of 1980. Pointing to the revitalized economy and a renewed sense of national pride, Reagan was now able to proclaim that it was "morning in America." He was again nominated by the Republican party. Vice-President George Bush was also renominated.

The Democratic nominee was Walter F. Mondale, the Minnesota Senator who had served as Jimmy Carter's Vice-President. Mondale's running mate was Congresswoman Geraldine Ferraro of New York, the first woman to be nomi-

Although they were soundly defeated by the incumbent President Reagan and Vice President Bush, the team of Walter Mondale and Geraldine Ferraro made history; Geraldine Ferraro was the first woman Vice-Presidential nominee of a major American political party.

nated for Vice-President by a major political party. Mondale ran on a platform of ''New Realism,'' in contrast to Reagan's ''New Federalism,'' and he declared his willingness to raise taxes to reduce the federal deficit. Once again, barely 50% of the electorate went to the polls; and, once again, Reagan won, this time in a landslide. Reagan captured not only a majority of the popular vote but a record 525 electoral votes. Mondale received a majority of the popular vote in only his native Minnesota and the Dis-

trict of Columbia. While Reagan's overwhelming victory confirmed his popularity, the elections also reestablished a solid Democratic majority in the Senate, somewhat diminishing the President's influence in the legislature.

Geneva, Reykjavik, and Washington

Relations between the United States and the Soviet Union had been cool during Reagan's first term. The deaths of three Soviet leaders between 1982 and 1985 had made attempts at communication between the two nations difficult. American-Soviet relations were further strained in September, 1983, when a Russian warplane shot down a Korean airliner that had strayed into Soviet airspace. Two hundred and sixty-nine passengers were killed, including 61 Americans. Arms-control talks were broken off in 1983 with no date set for reconvening. In 1984, the Soviet Union announced a boycott of the summer Olympic Games in Los Angeles in retaliation for Carter's American boycott of the 1980 Moscow Olympics. The low point in relations was reached in March, 1983, when President Reagan, angered at both the Soviet Union's support for Communist insurgency in the Third World and its continuing war in Afghanistan, gave a speech characterizing the Soviet Union as an "evil empire."

But by the mid-1980s, rapport between the two superpowers showed signs of improving. The Soviet Union had a new, dynamic leader, Mikhail Gorbachev. Gorbachev promised the Soviet people a program of *glasnost*— openness—embracing economic reform, increased tolerance of opposing viewpoints, and a greater respect for human rights. To the United States, Gorbachev extended a willingness to negotiate on issues such as arms control.

Both Gorbachev and *glasnost* were criticized as insincere and superficial by some American leaders, but popular support for arms-control negotiations led to a meeting between Reagan and Gorbachev in Geneva, Switzerland, on November 19 and 20, 1985. It was the first meeting between the President of the United States and a General Secretary of the Soviet Union in six years. The two leaders agreed on the idea of a 50% reduction of nuclear arms as a subject for future negotiations.

The discussions between Reagan and Gorbachev resumed at Reykjavik, Iceland, in October, 1986. At first, talks aimed at a new arms control agreement went well, but the negotiations stalled over the issue of the Strategic Defense Initiative (SDI). SDI, informally known as "Star Wars" in the American media, was the Reagan administration's plan for an impregnable defense against Soviet nuclear missiles, based on existing and projected technology. It was to rely on a vast system of satellites and lasers to provide an "umbrella" through which nuclear missiles could not pass without being destroyed. The $3-trillion project was to be the centerpiece of America's anti-missile defenses. Despite the fact that SDI could not be implemented until an undetermined point in the future, Reagan refused to compromise on it. The Reykjavik summit produced no specific arms-limitation agreements, but negotiating teams from the two nations continued work on the removal of short-range and medium-range missiles from Europe. Reagan and Gorbachev agreed to another summit meeting.

In December of 1987, Gorbachev arrived in Washington, and on December 8, the two leaders signed the Intermediate Nuclear Forces (INF) treaty. The treaty called for a reduction of medium-range missiles in Europe and provided

THE WHITE HOUSE

1572

for guaranteed verification of missile sites in the United States, the Soviet Union, and Western Europe for 13 years. It made no mention of President Reagan's SDI project. The INF treaty was not without its critics. Conservatives charged it removed a vital deterrent from Europe, and liberals and anti-nuclear activists felt that it marked a good beginning but did not go nearly far enough. However, the fact that the two most powerful men in the world, two ideological opposites, were able to sit down together and agree to reduce nuclear arms introduced a strong note of hope into a world troubled by the possibility of nuclear annihilation.

Other headline events

The nation was shocked on January 28, 1986, when the space shuttle *Challenger* exploded 73 seconds after lifting off from the Kennedy Space Center in Florida. Aboard the shuttle were six astronauts and a New Hampshire schoolteacher, Christa McAuliffe, who had been chosen as the first American civilian to go into space. Millions of people watched the tragedy on television, including thousands of schoolchildren who had expected to receive special

President Reagan is briefed by an arms-control negotiation team prior to the summit meeting between Reagan and Soviet General Secretary Mikhail Gorbachev in Washington, D.C., in December, 1987.

Lieutenant Colonel Oliver L. North, a decorated Marine and a high-ranking National Security Council official, was the center of the Iran-Contra Affair.

lessons broadcast to earth from the shuttle by McAuliffe. The *Challenger* disaster, the worst in the history of the American space program, provoked a nationwide outpouring of grief. At a special memorial service for the shuttle's crew, President Reagan praised their courage and commitment to space exploration. The *Challenger* tragedy was followed by the failure of several unmanned space vehicles, and the string of disasters set back the U.S. space program several years.

In 1986, the Reagan administration was rocked by revelations of serious misconduct by members of the White House's National Security Council. After reports began appearing in the press that the United States had secretly sold arms to Iran, Reagan ordered first his Attorney General and then a three-man investigating committee to look into the

matter. They found that top officers of the National Security Counsel, in the White House, had sought to win the release of American hostages in Lebanon by surrepetitiously selling arms to Iran, with profits from the sales going to aid the Contras in Nicaragua, circumventing Congress, which had outlawed both such sales and such aid. Televised Senate hearings on the affair in the summer of 1987 made an instant celebrity of Marine Lieutenant Colonel Oliver North, one of the plan's principle archtitects. Witnesses testifying before the committee, including many of Reagan's highest aides, gave conflicting accounts of how the affair had arisen and who had authorized it; President Reagan, in various ways and at various times, denied knowledge or sanction of such activities. Ultimately, he admitted supporting the secret arms sales to Iran but denied knowledge of the channeling of funds to the Contras. The investigating committee's revelations led to a revamping of the National Security Council to return it to an advisory rather than operational role, and the appointment of a special prosecutor to seek indictments for illegal acts that were part of the affair.

The Reagan Presidency also saw a number of changes in the personnel of the Supreme Court, including the appointment of the first woman Justice, Sandra Day O'Connor, the first Italian-American Justice, Antonin Scalia, and a new Chief Justice, William H. Rehnquist. In 1987, two Reagan nominees, Robert H. Bork and Douglas H. Ginsburg, were rejected by the Senate after unusually controversial hearings and investigations.

Americans were alarmed by the rapid spread of a new, deadly disease, AIDS (Acquired Immune Deficiency Syndrome), which made its first significant appearance in the United States in 1982. It proved to be spread mainly through sexual contact and shared hypodermic needles, and to afflict mainly homosexuals and intravenous drug users. Concern over AIDS led to calls for increased funding of medical research to find a cure and educational programs to slow its spread.

Millions of stockholders large and small received a shock when the boom-

On October 19, 1987—"Black Monday"—the Dow Jones Industrial average dropped a dizzying 508 points, prompting widespread concern over the stability of the American economy.

ing stock market collapsed abruptly on October 19, 1987, with the Dow Jones index dropping more than 508 points, the most dramatic one-day plunge ever. The market fluctuated widely on into December, when it began to show signs of stabilizing, but at a much lower level.

Two anniversaries

Since 1886, the Statue of Liberty has towered above New York harbor as a beacon of freedom and a symbol of the hope that America has held out to the oppressed peoples of the world. A century of wind and weather had damaged the Statue, and in the mid-1980s, a restoration program began, financed by

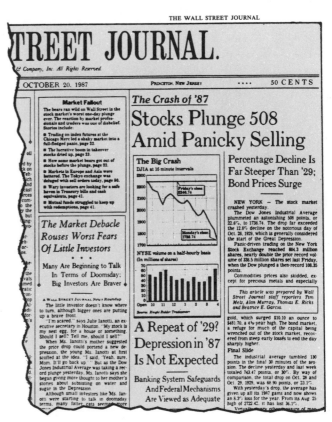

As housing costs skyrocketed, homelessness among Americans became a crisis of major proportions in the 1980s.

the contributions of both corporations and individual citizens. In July, 1986, celebrations marking the hundredth anniversary of the newly restored Statue were held in New York and around the nation. On Ellis Island, from whose halls the forebears of many Americans first entered the country, 38,000 new American citizens were sworn in, reminding the world that America is still a nation built on the hopes, dreams, and hard work of immigrants.

The summer of 1987 saw a nationwide celebration of the two-hundredth anniversary of the drafting and signing of the Constitution of the United States. For two hundred years—the longest duration of any national constitution—this remarkable document has safeguarded the rights and freedoms of Americans and provided a workable framework for democratic government. A striking counterpoint to the celebrations was provided by the Senate's televised hearings on the Iran-Contra affair. They proved anew that, two centuries after a handful of delegates had gathered in Philadelphia to hammer out a Constitution, the document they shaped is still very much alive, and still lies at the heart of the fundamental workings of our government.

A book compiled by The New York Times *detailed the findings of the several committees formed to investigate the Iran-Contra affair.*

AMERICAN CELEBRATES

In the 1970s and 1980s, Americans several times put aside the concerns of the present to commemorate the nation's past. Three great historical happenings were celebrated between 1975 and 1987—the Declaration of Independence, which had announced our freedom to the world, was 200 years old on July 4, 1976; The Bicentennial of the Constitution of the United States, which set the fundamental guidelines to insure that freedom, was marked by numerous events in 1987; and the Statue of Liberty, perhaps the best-known symbol of that freedom, received its one-hundredth birthday party in 1986.

It has been said that Americans love a parade, and these historic birthdays were celebrated with hundreds of parades—from simple marches on the main streets of countless small towns to the stately procession of tall ships up New York Harbor. And, of course, no American celebration would be complete without fireworks, bands, speeches, and flags. All three celebrations shared this enthusiasm, but each had its unique characteristics. At the ceremonies marking the hundredth birthday of the Statue of Liberty, thousands of immigrants were sworn in as new U.S. citizens—affirming, once again, that we are a nation of immigrants, with our strength coming from our diversity. The celebration of the Constitution's birthday took place amid fervent debate on the Senate Floor as to just how that document is to be interpreted in a rapidly changing America. And the Bicentennial of our country—coming as it did just after we had been severely tried with the domestic and foreign crises of the early 1970s—helped Americans summon the vision and strength to face the nation's third century with renewed hope and confidence.

AMERICA CELEBRATES

Tall sailing ships from around the world arrived in New York for OPSAIL, a nautical celebration of the nation's Bicentennial, as seen in this New York City subway poster.

President Ford, aboard the aircraft carrier USS Forrestal, initiates the Bicentennial festivities in New York Harbor by ringing a replica of the Liberty Bell. At his side is Secretary of the Navy John Warner.

The official commemorative seal of the United States Bicentennial.

NEW YORK CITY CONVENTION BUREAU

Witness Operatio
July 4, 1976, the tall ships s

PHOTO BY SUNNY SIT

AMERICAN REVOLUTION BICENTENNIAL 1776-1976

Sail, the greatest sailing event in New York history, to New York Harbor and up the Hudson River as part of our Bicentennial Celebration.

AMERICA CELEBRATES

This Currier & Ives lithograph (below) showed Americans how the Statue of Liberty, a gift from France to America, was to look when erected on Bedloe's (now Liberty) Island in New York Harbor. At right, U.S. Commemorative Stamp.

A sailboat glides through the waters of New York Harbor during "Liberty Weekend." Tourists from around the nation and the world poured into New York to help "Miss Liberty" celebrate her centennial.

1580

Crowds gather at the Capitol building in Washington, D.C., to mark the Bicentennial of the U.S. Constitution. The words "We the People" above the grandstand quote the opening of the document's preamble.

A huge American flag hangs from the Gateway Arch in St. Louis, Missouri, as the centerpiece of that city's celebration of the Bicentennial of the Constitution.

Warren Burger, Chief Justice of the Supreme Court from 1969 to 1986, became Chairman of the Committee on the Bicentennial of the U.S. Constitution immediately after leaving the Court. Above, he opens one of the many exhibits around the nation on the history of the Constitution.

Left, dancers and a fife-and-drum band celebrate the Statue of Liberty's Centennial at Walt Disney World.

Top right, sailors aboard the aircraft carrier U.S.S. Ranger spell out the Constitution's opening words on maneuvers off the California Coast in April, 1987.

Right, a float built by the Girl Scouts of Nevada City, CA. commemorates the Constitution at a parade in September, 1987.

COURTESY OF THE COMMISSION ON THE BICENTENNIAL OF THE U.S. CONSTITUTION

Mayor Harold Washington of Chicago, top left, rings the New Freedom Bell in Daley Plaza, Chicago, on May 12, 1987.

Left, dressed in the uniforms of the Continental Army, "The Commander-In Chief's Guard" of Orange County, Virginia fire a salute to James Madison, the Constitution's principle architect, on the 236 anniversary of his birth, March 15, 1987.

Above, six-hundred students of the Mayfield, New York Central High School form a human map of the United States on September 16, 1987.

Right, a gathering in Los Angeles, California hears a speech. The grandstand is a replica of the chairs in Independence Hall, Philadelphia, with the "rising sun" design made famous by Benjamin Franklin.

A Few Parchment Pages Two Hundred Years Later

A SPECIAL CONTRIBUTION BY

RICHARD B. MORRIS

The framers of the Constitution were proud of what they had done but might be astonished that their words still carry so much weight. A distinguished scholar tells us how the great charter has survived and flourished.

The American Constitution has functioned and endured longer than any other written constitution of the modern era. It imbues the nation with energy to act while restraining its agents from acting improperly. It safeguards our liberties and establishes a government of laws, not of men and women. Above all, the Constitution is the mortar that binds the fifty-state edifice under the concept of federalism; it is the symbol that unifies nearly 250,000,000 people of different origins, races, and religions into a single nation.

Over two centuries dozens of constitutions adopted in other countries have gone into the scrap heap. The United States Constitution has

On September 17, 1787, the delegates to the Constitutional Convention put quill pen to parchment and adopted the Constitution of the United States, the document which, two centuries later, still guides our nation.

outlived almost all its successors. The longevity of the Constitution makes us wonder whether its thirty-nine signers planned it that way, and if they did, why doesn't the Constitution declare itself to be perpetual, unlike the weak "perpetual" union—the Articles of Confederation—that it succeeded? Somehow the adjective was overlooked in the federal convention, while the word *compact* was deliberately avoided in a vain attempt to forestall the issue of whether the Constitution was a compact between the states, which any party could disavow, or between the government and the people, which States' Righters might have found unacceptable.

However, the Constitution does start with a hint that it was aiming for longevity. The Preamble, in Gouverneur Morris's incomparable language, says that its purpose is "to form a more perfect Union" and "secure the Blessings of Liberty to ourselves and our Posterity. . . ." President Washington in his Farewell Address speaks of the "efficacy and permanency of your union." Nevertheless, both the supremacy and the permanence of the Constitution were to be challenged within a decade. To oppose the Alien and Sedition Acts of 1798, which curbed the actions of hostile aliens and held the press criminally accountable for "false" and "malicious" writings about the government, James Madison and Thomas Jefferson joined forces to write the Kentucky and Virginia Resolutions. These asserted that a state had the power to "interpose"

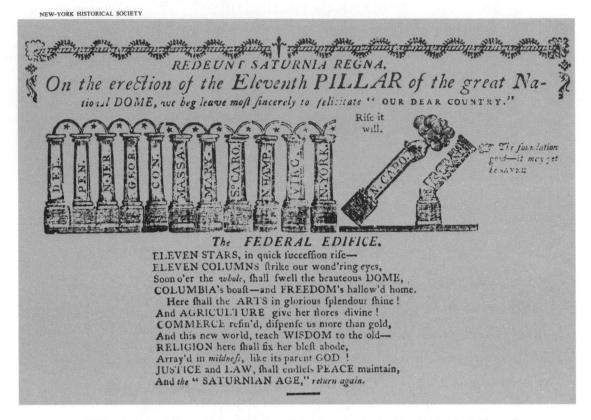

REDEUNT SATURNIA REGNA.

On the erection of the Eleventh PILLAR of the great National DOME, we beg leave most sincerely to felicitate "OUR DEAR COUNTRY."

The FEDERAL EDIFICE.

ELEVEN STARS, in quick succession rise—
ELEVEN COLUMNS strike our wond'ring eyes,
Soon o'er the *whole*, shall swell the beauteous DOME,
COLUMBIA's boast—and FREEDOM's hallow'd home.
Here shall the ARTS in glorious splendour shine !
And AGRICULTURE give her stores divine !
COMMERCE refin'd, dispense us more than gold,
And this new world, teach WISDOM to the old—
RELIGION here shall fix her blest abode,
Array'd in *mildness*, like its parent GOD !
JUSTICE and LAW, shall endless PEACE maintain,
And *the* " SATURNIAN AGE," *return again*.

A 1788 cartoon celebrates the ratification of the Constitution by New York—the "Eleventh Pillar" of the new "Federal Edifice."

when the government exceeded its powers as enumerated in the Constitution.

By 1828, the challenge of "interposition" had become the threat of "nullification" when John C. Calhoun endorsed South Carolina's refusal to obey a new tariff measure. In spite of vigorous support by Daniel Webster and President Andrew Jackson, the life-span of the Constitution seemed jeopardized on the eve of the Civil War as "nullification" gave way to "secession," and the Southern states claimed that the Constitution was dissoluble at the pleasure of any state that might wish to secede.

Confronted by a burgeoning secessionist movement, President Lincoln declared, "I hold that, in contemplation of universal law and of the Constitution, the Union of these States is perpetual." The word was out at last. The Union forged by the

Constitution could not be dismantled. To put the issue beyond controversy required four years of war and a Supreme Court decision to settle the question of whether the Constitution was a compact of *sovereign states* or a compact of the *people of the states*, as was originally intended. The Supreme Court confirmed the military decision, denying the right of states to secede. In *Texas v. White* in 1869, it declared, "The Constitution, in all its provisions, looks to an indestructible Union, composed of indestructible States."

One of the clues to the mystery of the Constitution's durability is the plastic quality that makes it applicable to a rapidly changing society. At the convention, it was the Committee of Detail's deliberate intention, in the words of its draftsman, Edmund Randolph, "to insert essential principles only" in order to accommodate the Constitution "to times and events" and "to use simple and precise language, and general propositions. . . ." Randolph's notion of confining a constitution to broad principles was a masterstroke that contributed immensely to that document's enduring suitability and relevance, and James Wilson of Pennsylvania contributed further by putting Randolph's draft into smoother prose. Finally, the Committee of Style and Arrangement, under the swift and sure guidance of Gouverneur Morris and his talented colleagues, gave us the final draft, a masterpiece of conciseness.

How different, indeed, from most modern state constitutions, which are often hugely long with their general principles buried under a heap of minute local and transitory details. The great charter, a few parchment pages adopted in 84 working days, is a broad blueprint of governance, timeless in character.

Another aspect of the working methods of the framers helps explain the relatively speedy adoption and ratification of the Constitution. In 1839, on the fiftieth anniversary of the establishment of the national government, John Quincy Adams spoke of the federal Constitution as having been "extorted" from the "grinding necessity of a reluctant nation." He was attesting to the fact that only a combination of bold innovation, compromise, and concession made it possible to frame and ratify the Constitution. Adams may well have been overstating the case, for in fact, the overwhelming majority of the delegates to the Philadelphia convention were nationalists of one sort or another, convinced of the need to confer a taxing power on a central government, to invest it with jurisdiction over foreign and interstate commerce, and to establish a framework that would be the supreme law of the land.

Within this extraordinary company of statesmen, there developed sharp differences about how such a constitution could be made to conform to truly republican principles, how vestiges of sovereignty could be left to the states, just what powers should be enumerated to the national (or federal) government, and how far the states could be restrained. The result was a series of compromises and concessions, some minor and easily settled, some major and involving prolonged debate.

School texts invariably refer to the Great Compromise by which the small states gained equality in the Senate while the House of Representatives was made proportional to the population. But even within that compromise, credited to the Connecticut delegates, there were additional compromises. Once it was settled that the House was to be elected by the people, the issue arose as to how the Senate was to be elected—also by the people, as the democratic nationalist James Wilson proposed; or by the House, as Edmund Randolph recommended; or by the state legislatures, an idea set forth by John Dickinson. The last suggestion was the one adopted, and it was a tribute to the delegates' concern about setting up a federal rather than a national constitution, thereby recognizing that certain powers inhered to the states. The Senate represented the states, and Article V of the Constitution guaranteed that no state could be deprived of equal suffrage in the Senate. This equality of the 50 states is a cardinal element of our federal system, reinforced by the Tenth Amendment, according to which "the powers not delegated to the United States by the Constitution, nor prohibited by it to the States, are reserved to the States, respectively, or to the people."

On the issue of choosing Senators, James Wilson's vision proved the sharpest, for the Senate came in later years to be perceived as a tool of the big business interests that tended to dominate the state legislatures. The Seventeenth Amendment, which was ratified in 1913, provided for direct election of Senators by the people, vindicating Wilson's original judgment.

While the large states won proportional representation in the House, the Northern states could hardly be expected to permit the South to count blacks, who were not eligible to vote, for purposes of that representation. Nor did the South care to include its slave population in the head count that would determine the amount of taxes it would have to pay in direct taxation. The result: Another compromise by which representation and direct taxes in the lower house would be based on "free persons," including servants bound for a term of years (a favored labor source of white labor in the tobacco states of Maryland and Virginia), and three-fifths of all other persons, "excluding Indians not taxed. . . ." As a result, in counting population, a black was included as three-fifths of a white person. The compromise gave something to each side: for the South, more Southerners to be represented in Congress; for the North, more heads to tax.

If the Great Compromise resolved differences between the states about representation, the second major compromise resulted from a confrontation between North and South about commerce. Everyone had agreed that conferring power over commerce upon the national government, along with the power to tax, was a prime motive for calling the convention. But the South now had second thoughts. States that shipped farm staples to a world market believed that this would work to the advantage of the North—which was heavily engaged in trade and shipping—while adding disproportionate costs to Southern exporters. To protect themselves against possible discrimination, some in the South sought to require a two-thirds vote in each house for passage of commercial legislation. The scholarly and creative James Madison, rising above sectional prejudices, prevailed upon the convention to reject this proposal and to give Congress the power to regulate commerce by a simple majority vote.

Nonetheless, every regional concession brought its price and begot its compromise. Thus, the great slavery issue came to the fore when the delegates took up the matter of import and export duties. The South proposed that Congress be forbidden from levying a tax on the importation of slaves or from prohibiting their importation altogether. Virginians, who were finding slavery less profitable than did their more southerly neighbors, did not join the Southern bloc. Nevertheless, over the objections of Virginia's great libertarian George Mason and of a divided North, the delegates worked out a compromise whereby no prohibition on the importation of "such persons as any of the states now existing shall think proper to admit" could be permitted before the year 1808. Even the North was split on this crucial and emotional vote. Nor was there a solid South.

In this way was slavery acknowledged, though not by name in the Constitution, and confirmed in two other compromises: the three-fifths rule for representation to the House of Representatives and for direct taxes and the provision for the return to their owners of fugitive persons "held to Service or Labor. . . ."

And the Philadelphia delegates continued to compromise. First, it was decided that the chief executive was to be a single person, not a committee or plural executive, as previously had been proposed. He would serve for four years (other proposals had ranged from a life term to a single seven-year term), and he was to be eligible for reelection. He would have a qualified veto (one that could be overridden by the legislative branch), not the absolute veto that some had urged. He would not be chosen by Congress, as the Virginia Plan had proposed, or selected directly by the people, as James Wilson would have preferred. Instead, the final decision, after countless proposals, was to have the President elected by electors who would be chosen in each state "in such a Manner" as its legislators might "direct." This plan perhaps conceived to propitiate the states, proved instead a victory for both nationalism and democracy, for very shortly after 1789, nearly all the state legislators provided for the election of their states' presidential electors by popular vote. If no candidate had a majority of the electoral vote, the ultimate choice would be made from the five highest candidates by the House of Representatives. However, in choosing the President, the House would vote by states, each state having one vote. Thus, the electoral college proved to be a compromise whereby the people, at least indirectly, would make the choice rather than the state legislatures.

Perhaps the ablest defense of all these compromises and concessions was made in *The Federalist*, in which Madison, while conceding that the Constitution was not a "faultless" document, admitted that the convention's delegates "were either satisfactorily accommodated by the final act; or were induced to accede to it out of a deep conviction of the *necessity of sacrificing private opinions* and *partial interests* to the *public good*, and by a despair of seeing this necessity diminished by the delays or by new experiments."

Finally, and certainly most important in terms of the safeguards for the people, the chief criticism leveled against the Constitution, when it was finally submitted for ratification, was the failure to incorporate a bill of rights. In ratifying the Constitution, a number of states included bills of rights among their recommendations. To ensure such compliance, New York even urged that a

George Washington, hero of the Revolution and the new nation's ablest leader, presided over the Convention.

second convention be called. The prospect of another convention, which might very well undo the great work already accomplished, appalled James Madison. Once elected to the House of Representatives, the Virginian reduced more than two hundred proposed amendments to twelve, of which ten were ratified. The Bill of Rights, as those first ten amendments are called, proved to be the great concession that quieted public fears about the new government's guarantees of civil liberties. This concession was Madison's noblest heritage to the nation.

If there was controversy from the very start about the scope and intent of the Constitution, that controversy has continued down to the present day. In fact, it has heated up over the current insistence by some legal minds that the Supreme Court in interpreting the Constitution is bound by the intent of the framers. This question addresses the public's conception of the Constitution: Is it a charter carved in stone or a malleable document that can be interpreted in response to rapidly changing moral and social values and

economic and technological demands? When Hamilton described the Constitution as looking "forward to remote futurity," how flexible did he consider it to be?

Are courts bound by the debates at the convention and the state ratifying conventions, or are they bound by the "express words" of the Constitution, and are we talking about the meaning of those words in 1787 or in the 1980s? Certainly the meaning that the drafters wished to communicate may differ from the meaning the reader is warranted to derive from the text.

What we do know, in studying the notes of debates on the framing of the Constitution, is that the framers' expected the Constitution to be interpreted in accord with its *express language*. "Vague" or "indefinite" language was criticized, and there were debates then and to this day as to how much of the war-making power was given to the President and how much to Congress.

Since the proceedings of the convention were secret and mostly not published until after James Madison's death some fifty years later, there is no possibility that the framers wished future interpreters to extract intention from their private debates. Nevertheless, in the debates over ratification, the Antifederalists expressed worries that the Congress and the federal judiciary would construe broadly the enumerated powers. At the New York ratification convention, John Jay sought to allay these fears by insisting that the document involved "no sophistry, no construction, no false glosses, but simple inference from the obvious operation of things." And Madison took pains to point out that improper construction of the Constitution could be remedied through amendment or by election "of more faithful representatives to annul the acts of the usurpers."

One of the most revealing examples of determining the intent of the framers occurred in their own later arguments about the "necessary and proper" clause. Article I, Section 8 lists among the powers granted Congress: "To make all Laws which shall be necessary and proper for carrying into Execution the foregoing Powers, and all other Powers vested by this Constitution in the Government of the United States, or in any Department or Officer thereof." Now it so happens that both James Madison and Alexander Hamilton served on the Committee of Style that was responsible for the final wording of the Constitution. In *The Federalist,* No. 44, Madison argued for a liberal interpretation of the "necessary and proper" clause in a way that must have delighted Hamilton, who was later to take the same position in defending the creation of the First Bank of the United States. The convention had, in fact, rejected a proposal to give Congress explicit power to charter corporations. Only after Madison had become involved with Jefferson in what amounted to the opposition party's assault on Hamilton's financial policies did Madison in effect repudiate his *Federalist* position and adopt the theory of "strict construction."

Yet it was to be Hamilton's interpretation of the scope of the "necessary and proper" clause that President Washington accepted and that Chief Justice John Marshall later embraced. Indeed, Hamilton anticipated the later assumption by the Supreme Court of powers for the federal government on the basis of three clauses of the Constitution, which, in addition to the "necessary and proper" clause, included the general welfare clause—granting Congress power "to provide for the . . . general Welfare of the United States"— and the commerce clause, giving Congress the power to "regulate Commerce with foreign Nations, and among the several States, and with the Indian Tribes. . . ." There is no question that we today owe to the vision of the framers a Constitution that can accommodate the modern welfare state under the general welfare clause and manufacturing within the commerce clause.

In *The Federalist,* No. 37, Madison, then sharing Hamilton's views, argued that the "intent" of any legal document is the product of the interpretive process, not of some fixed meaning that the author locks into the document's text at the outset. He ventured so far as to declare that even the meaning of God's Word "is rendered dim and doubtful by the cloudy medium through which it is communicated" when He "condescends to address mankind in their own language. . . ." It was up to the courts, Hamilton argued in a later *Federalist* letter, to fix the meaning and operation of laws, including the Constitution, and the courts could be expected to use the "rules of *common sense*" to determine the "natural and obvious sense" of the Constitution's provisions.

The question of the intention of the Philadelphia framers came up in one of the first great and controversial decisions handed down by the Supreme Court presided over by John Jay. *Chisholm v. Georgia* (1793) raised the question: Could a state be sued by a private citizen of another state? The language of the Constitution was, to say the least, ambiguous; according to Article III, federal judicial power could extend to controversies "between a State and Citizens of another State. . . ." In the debates on ratification, the framers went to great pains to deny that the Constitution would affect the state's sovereign immunity. Even Hamilton gave such assurances in *The Federalist,* No. 81. Yet a majority of the Court, construing the wording of Article III, held that the text was

Independence Hall in Philadelphia was the site of the signing of the Declaration of Independence as well as of the Constitution.

intended to *allow* suits against a state. But Georgia did not think so, and few amendments overruling a Supreme Court decision were adopted more speedily than the Eleventh Amendment, which in 1798, upheld the states' immunity to such actions.

How much weight did James Madison, often called the "father of the Constitution," give to the original intent of the framers? Very little, it seems, if we can judge from his insistence in his later years that "as a guide to expounding and applying the provisions of the Constitution, the debates and incidental decisions of the Convention can have no authoritative character." What counted in Madison's eyes were precedents derived from "authoritative, deliberate and continued decisions." Madison, who had originally phrased the Bill of Rights, sought to bind the states as well as Congress—a phrasing that mysteriously disappeared from the final product, which speaks only of Congress. He would have rejoiced at the modern Supreme Court's interpretation of the truly revolutionary Fourteenth Amendment, ratified in 1868 during the Reconstruction Era, and holding that the states as well as the federal government are bound by the Bill of Rights.

Indeed, what has contributed to the durability of the Constitution is its capacity to adapt to a society so different from that of the Founding Fathers. Shortly before the Constitutional Convention assembled, a mob put an alleged witch to death in Philadelphia, and just a few weeks later most of the delegates went down to the banks of the Delaware to see a demonstration of John Fitch's steamboat—so incongruous were the boundaries of knowledge at that time. A First Amendment setting up a wall of separation between church and state and guaranteeing freedom of religion was adopted by a people who were already facing one of the great fundamentalist religious revivals of our history.

A tour guide leads a group of tourists through the room in Independence Hall, where, in 1787, the Constitution was signed.

The Constitution made provision for such adjustments. Even though the word *equality* is missing in that seminal charter, in time amendments were adopted that, among other things, ended slavery (ratified in 1865), provided for "the equal protection of the laws" and "due process of law" for all persons (ratified 1868); conferred voting rights regardless of "race, color, or previous condition of servitude" (ratified 1870); required the direct election of Senators (ratified 1913); gave women the suffrage (ratified 1920); ended the poll tax as a bar to voting in federal elections (ratified 1964); and extended the suffrage to eighteen-year-olds (ratified 1971).

But not by amendments alone has the Constitution been reshaped. Actions of the three branches of government have broadened its text and applied its principles to specific situations only dimly perceived by the framers. As early as George Washington's administration, the principle of executive privilege was upheld, the rights of the President to dismiss appointees accepted, the cabinet—not mentioned in the Constitution—created, the right of the President to declare neutrality without consulting the Senate established, and the House of Representatives' power to withhold appropriations for treaties it did not approve of overruled. Finally, there emerged a party system—a system that none of the Founding Fathers anticipated—that Washington deplored in his Farewell Address, and that was considered a cause of faction and divisiveness. Yet today, political parties are accepted as the touchstone of a democratic society, and the repression of opposition parties as one of the most visible symptoms of a totalitarian state.

Despite these enlargements and glosses upon the original Constitution made by both the President and Congress over the past two centuries, it is the High Court that bears the brunt of criticism for straying from the intent of the framers. Critics charge the Supreme Court with practicing what amounts to judicial legislation to effect due process, achieve equal justice, assure voting equality, and maintain the right of privacy even in cases in which it is dubious that a majority of the nation's citizens support some of its advanced positions.

In 1787 and 1788, and again today, critics contend that judges, who are insulated from the electorial process, should not be entrusted with final interpretation of the laws. But no federal judge has ever been impeached and removed from the bench because his decisions have run counter to public opinion. Only on grounds of "high crimes or misdemeanors"—not deviation from prevailing political norms—is a federal judge liable to impeachment and removal. To Alexander Hamilton, the independence of the judicial branch was essential if the courts were to maintain their role as guardian of the Constitution's limits on power.

That independence is the central issue concerning the federal judiciary's role today. The Supreme Court is increasingly preoccupied with cases that deal with social and moral issues—the death penalty, desegregation, school busing, prayer in schools, abortion, privacy—and litigants insist that the justices fill the vacuum created by the lack of direction on these subjects from the two other branches of government that, unlike the Court, are subject to the electoral process.

No single branch of the government can long evade the issue of accountability for interpreting the Constitution. The President fills vacancies on the Court, usually picking persons who reflect his constitutional views. In requiring the President to swear to "preserve, protect and defend the Constitution," the public expects him to determine if and when it is being threatened. Some Presidents, like Lincoln, looked neither to Congress nor to the courts in times of crisis. Deciding that the Union was indissoluble, Lincoln explicitly assumed the authority and took on the full burden of maintaining the Union.

Nor can Congress escape responsibility, since it is charged by the Constitution with enacting regulations concerning the Supreme Court's jurisdiction except when spelled out in Article III. Beginning with the Judiciary Act of 1789, Congress has set the parameters of the federal courts' jurisdiction and within those constitutional limitations can enlarge or diminish the scope of litigation that may be brought to trial in the federal courts.

Finally, we the people have the power of defining the Constitution through the ballot box, albeit that power has seldom been used directly to affect judicial decisions. The most startling exception was in 1936, when, not long after the election, the Supreme Court in obvious response to public opinion began to yield to the President's and Congress's constitutional views. But that example was dramatic and virtually without parallel. Indeed, few citizens consciously or systematically utilize their ballots to register constitutional interpretations. This omission leaves officials to resolve most conflicts themselves, but Senators, Representatives, and Presidents do so, subject to the disapproval of voters, whereas the Court is politically unaccountable.

True, the Constitution contains a provision for amendment by calling a convention, but the framers, having themselves violated their instructions by overthrowing rather than revising the Articles of Confederation, were loath to expose their great work to a second convention. And despite the number of states that in recent years have gone on record to call for such a second convention, the wording of the calls are varied and imprecise and the dangers to the durable structure of the nation seem too great to bear the risk.

In the landmark case of *Cohens v. Virginia* (1821), Chief Justice John Marshall spoke of a constitution as having been "framed for ages to come" and as being "designed to approach immortality as nearly as human institutions can approach it." These remain appropriate words for the Constitution after its bicentennial celebration. An issue-laden document, always a storm center of dissent, the Constitution is, praradoxically, still held in affection, even veneration, by the people of America.

In the years ahead, it should continue to function so long as it can meet the objectives that were set forth in the preamble in the name of "We the People": to "insure domestic Tranquillity, provide for the common defence, promote the general Welfare, and secure the Blessings of Liberty to ourselves and our Posterity. . . ." For more than two hundred complex years, it has remained steadfast to these goals. No worthier aims can be set for the great charter as it continues into its third century.

Richard B. Morris is Gouverneur Morris, Professor of History at Columbia University, and the author of many books, the most recent of which is Forging of the Union, 1781-1789, *published by Harper & Row.*

Volume 18
ENCYCLOPEDIC SECTION

The two-page reference guide below lists the entries by categories. The entries in this section supplement the subject matter covered in the text of this volume. A **cross-reference** (*see*) means that a separate entry appears elsewhere in this section. However, certain important persons and events mentioned here have individual entries in the Encyclopedic Sections of other volumes. Consult the Index in this Volume.

AMERICAN PRESIDENTS, STATESMEN AND POLITICIANS

John Anderson	Jesse Jackson
Howard Baker	Walter Mondale
George Bush	Sandra Day O'Connor
Jimmy Carter	Thomas P. ("Tip") O'Neill
William Casey	Ronald Reagan
Elizabeth Dole	William Rehnquist
Robert Dole	George Shultz
Geraldine Ferraro	David Stockman
Alexander Haig	Caspar Weinberger

SCIENCE AND TECHNOLOGY

AIDS   **The *Challenger* Disaster**

DOMESTIC AFFAIRS

Amnesty International   **Lee Iacocca**
Baby M. Case   **P.A.C.'s**
Equal Rights Amendment   **The Religious Right**
Farm Failures   **Right to Life/Pro-Choice Controversy**
The Homeless in America   **Wall Street Volatility**
Immigration

FOREIGN AFFAIRS

Corazon Aquino   **INF Treaty**
Leonid Brezhnev   **Pope John Paul II**
Mikhail Gorbachev   **Libya**
Grenada   **Nicaragua**
Haiti   **Palestine Liberation Organization**
Iran-Contra Affair   **South Africa/Apartheid**
Iran Hostage Crisis   **Margaret Thatcher**

SPORTS AND CULTURE

Hank Aaron   **Saul Bellow**

A

AARON, Henry Louis (born 1934). On April 8, 1974, Hank Aaron hit his record 715th home run, marking not only a personal triumph but a symbol of the successful integration of the American pastime which had begun just 27 years earlier with the introduction of Jackie Robinson (1919-1972) to the Brooklyn Dodgers' lineup. Born and raised in Mobile, Alabama, Aaron first played professionally in 1952 on an all-black team in the waning days of the Negro Leagues, once the only leagues in which black ballplayers could play. Later that year, the National League's Boston Braves signed him to a contract. After brief stops on minor league teams in Eau Claire, Wisconsin, and Jacksonville, Florida, Aaron became in 1954 the starting rightfielder for the Braves—who had by then moved to Milwaukee, Wisconsin. For the next 20 years, Aaron was a fixture in the Braves' outfield (he also played a few games at every infield position except shortstop). Although he made his lasting mark as a home-run hitter, Aaron excelled in every area of the sport. Named the National League's Most Valuable Player in 1957, Aaron led the league in batting average twice (.328 in 1956 and .355 in 1959), in runs batted in four times (1957, 1960, 1963, and 1966), and in runs scored three times (1957, 1963, and 1967); he won three consecutive Gold Glove Awards (1958-1960) for fielding excellence; and he averaged 22 stolen bases a year from 1960 to 1968. But these formidable skills were overshadowed by his incredible ability to hit home runs. Although he led the league in home runs only four times (1957, 1963, 1966, and 1967) and never reached 50 in a single season—primarily because his best years were spent in cavernous Milwaukee County Stadium—before the Braves moved again in 1966, this time to Atlanta, Georgia—Aaron's consistency and

Hank Aaron

durability left him by the end of 1973 just one shot behind the career leader Babe Ruth (1895-1948). Aaron tied Ruth's record of 714 lifetime home runs on April 4, 1974, in Cincinnati, Ohio, during the first game of the season. In the Braves' first home game, on April 8, he powered a fastball thrown by Los Angeles Dodger pitcher Al Downing (born 1941)—who, like Aaron, wore uniform number 44—into the left-field bleachers. Aaron ended his playing career with the Milwaukee Brewers, retiring in 1976 with a .305 lifetime batting average, career records in home runs (755), runs batted in (2,297), games played (3,298), and at bats (12,364), and trailing only Ty Cobb (1886-1961) in runs scored (2,174) and hits (3,771). Although Pete Rose (born 1941) would later surpass Aaron's (and Cobb's) records in games, at-bats, runs, and hits, Hank Aaron easily won a place among baseball's immortals and was inducted into the Baseball Hall of Fame on August 1, 1982. Aaron has continued to serve the game he loved as Director of Player Development for the Atlanta Braves, and as late as 1987—forty years after the playing fields themselves were integrated—he was the only black executive in major-league baseball.

AIDS (Acquired Immune Deficiency Syndrome). Acquired Immune Deficiency Syndrome first appeared among homosexual men in New York and California in 1980. By the end of 1987, Aids had taken the lives of over 20,000 Americans and afflicted almost 50,000 others. AIDS is very difficult to transmit, but very powerful once inside the body. The infection is passed from one person to another through intimate sexual contact, use of a contaminated needle by intravenous drug users, from mother to fetus, and from the transfusion of contaminated blood. The AIDS virus attacks the body's white blood cells. Since these cells are fundamental in warding off outside infections, AIDS makes the immune system more vulnerable to other diseases such as pneumonia, which is the major cause of death among AIDS victims. Even though AIDS cannot be transmitted by any kind of casual social contact such as shaking hands or going to school with AIDS patients, fear and concern over AIDS has led Federal and state governments to pass legislation requiring various persons to be tested for the AIDS virus and to consider the right of confidentiality for persons carrying the AIDS virus. Also, mandatory AIDS testing is required for all immigrants hoping to become citizens. While no specific cure or vaccine for AIDS has been found, scientists have used a drug called azidothymidine (AZT) to extend the lives of AIDS patients.

AMNESTY INTERNATIONAL. Amnesty International was founded in 1961 to protect human rights around the world. It seeks the release of all prisoners of conscience. These are people detained anywhere for their beliefs, color, sex, ethnic origin, language, or religion, who have not used or advocated violence. It works for fair and prompt trials for all political prisoners, and on behalf of people detained without charge or trial. It opposes the death penalty and torture or other cruel, inhuman, and degrading punishment for all prisoners. Amnesty International has more than 700,000 members in over 150 countries. It has more than 3,800 local groups, most of which are organized into Amnesty International sections in 46 countries. In 1986, Amnesty attracted the attention of many Americans, especially young people, when a number of popular rock and folk artists joined forces on a highly successful nationwide tour called the "Conspiracy of Hope" to publicize Amnesty International's activities, raise funds, and increase membership. Amnesty's work is impartial and concerned solely with the protection of human rights, regardless of the ideology of the governments and the beliefs of the victims in each case. It attaches great importance to impartial and accurate reporting of facts. The organization's Research Department, located at its International Secretariat in London, England, collects and analyzes information from a large variety of sources, including fact-finding missions and trial observations. In March, 1988, Amnesty International was following the cases of 3,400 prisoners of conscience, seeking the most effective means of helping individuals whose rights had been violated. Amnesty applies a variety of techniques, including long-term "adoption" of prisoners of conscience by local groups of members, publicizing of patterns of human rights abuses, and, in cases where torture or death is feared, a network of volunteers who send telegrams expressing international concern. Persistent actions like these often generate effective pressure on repressive governments. Amnesty members also organize public meetings, collect signatures for petitions, and arrange publicity events such as vigils at appropriate government agencies. They work on special projects, such as the Campaign to Abolish Torture. Since Amnesty was founded it has taken up the cases of more than 30,000 prisoners. In 1977, Amnesty International received the Nobel Peace Prize for its efforts. In the United States, Amnesty has raised awareness of human rights violations abroad by extensive programs in schools where students launch letter-writing campaigns on behalf of prisoners of conscience. Such programs are practical ways of showing students that freedom of expression and opinion, rights we as Americans take for granted, are often nonexistent in other nations.

ANDERSON, John B. (born 1922). Although he failed to win a single electoral vote, John Anderson gained almost 7% of the popular vote as a Republican who bolted from his party and ran as an independent in the 1980 presidential election. Born in 1922 in Rockford, Illinois, the son of a Swedish immigrant store owner, Anderson received a B.A. degree in political science from the University of Illinois in 1942, then served in the U.S. Army during World War II. He received law degrees from the University of Illinois College of Law in 1946 and from Harvard University in 1949, then practiced law in Illinois. In 1960, he ran for a vacant Congressional seat and was elected by a decisive margin. He was a conservative in his first years in Congress, and supported Barry M. Goldwater (born 1909) for President in 1964. Beginning in the mid-1960s, perhaps partly in response to an influx of liberal blue-collar voters in his home district, Anderson moderated his positions, supporting increased educational aid and food-stamp programs, for example, and actively promoting the 1968 open-housing law. A supporter of President Richard Nixon's (born 1913) domestic policies, Anderson was sharply critical of his "phased troop withdrawal" from Vietnam. During the unraveling of the **Watergate** scandal (*see*), Anderson was one of the first Republicans to speak out against President Nixon, co-sponsoring a bill calling for the appointment of a special prosecutor in May, 1973, and later urging the President to resign three months before he actually did. Anderson continued to serve in Congress until 1980, perplexing political analysts who attempted to typecast him by voting liberally on social welfare issues (winning a 55% rating from the liberal lobbying organization Americans for Democratic Action), but conservatively on many economic issues (earning a 44% rating from the conservative Americans for Constitutional Action). After finishing poorly in the Republican Presidential primary campaigns of 1980, he ran as a third-party candidate in the general election, shaping his appeal to moderate Republicans and Democrats disenchanted with President Carter. Although he had to fight for media coverage, Anderson's share of the popular vote provided the difference between Reagan and Carter in fourteen states.

AQUINO, Corazon Cojuangco (born 1933). A reluctant public figure forced into politics when her husband was assassinated, Aquino led the democratic revolution that ousted Philippine dictator Ferdinand E. Marcos (born 1917), who had ruled for 20 years. After becoming President of the Philippines in 1986, Aquino dismantled the remnants of the Marcos regime and oversaw the transition to a constitutional democracy. Born into a wealthy sugar-plantation-owning family fifty miles north of the capital city of Manila, Maria Corazon Cojuangco was sent to the United States at age thirteen to attend Catholic convent schools and graduated from Mount St. Vincent College in the Bronx, New York, in 1953. A year later, she left law school in Manila to marry Benigno Aquino, Jr. (1932-1983), a young journalist. For the next 18 years, she concentrated on raising their five children while her husband, pursued a career in Philippine politics as a vocal opponent of President Marcos.

In 1972, Marcos—prolonging his presidency beyond the legally allowed two terms—declared martial law and arrested opposition leaders, among them Benigno Aquino. Corazon Aquino was her imprisoned husband's only contact with the outside world until 1980, when, under pressure from United States President **Jimmy Carter** (*see*), Marcos released Benigno Aquino and allowed him to travel to the United States for heart surgery. Following his surgery, Benigno Aquino accepted academic positions at Harvard University and the Massachusetts Institute of Technology; three years later he decided to return home to help the opposition party prepare for the next elections. On August 21, 1983, as he stepped from the plane that had brought him to the Manila International Airport, Benigno Aquino was shot and killed. Although the Marcos government claimed to have killed the assassin responsible for the slaying, eyewitnesses reported that government soldiers had actually shot Benigno Aquino. Corazon Aquino presided over her husband's funeral procession, attended by over a million people—wearing yellow as a symbol of her husband's martyrdom—led the opposition that finally brought about Marcos's downfall. An economic downturn and the rising number of Communist insurgents in Filipino provinces prompted President **Ronald Reagan** (*see*) to pressure Marcos to institute wide-ranging reforms. In November, 1985, Marcos announced plans for a new presidential election. After receiving petitions with over a million signatures urging her to run, and after learning that the conviction of the military officers involved in her husband's murder had been overturned, Aquino announced her candidacy. Aquino unified the dispersed opposition to the Marcos regime and offered herself to the Filipino people as a moral alternative to the corruption and repression that had characterized Marcos's reign. Following a

February 7, 1986, election marred by stolen ballot boxes, bribes, and harassment of voters, both Marcos and Aquino claimed victory. On February 22, Marcos's defense minister and his armed forces deputy chief of staff announced their support of Aquino, throwing the weight of the military behind the opposition candidate. On February 25, both candidates staged inaugurations, but Marcos—heeding the advice of U.S. officials—immediately fled the country for the United States, ultimately settling in Hawaii. Although inexperienced in government and faced with the dire economic and political problems left behind by Marcos, Aquino quickly took charge, forming a coalition of moderate business leaders, restoring political rights, and releasing hundreds of political prisoners—including prominent Communist leaders, much to the chagrin of her military advisers. On March 25, 1986, she declared a transitional government—giving herself the right to rule by fiat until a new democratic constitution could be drafted. Aquino's reassurance that her country would allow the United States to maintain its two Philippine military bases until at least 1991 won her the support of the Reagan administration, a commitment reinforced during her nine-day trip to the United States in September, 1986. After hearing Aquino deliver what House Speaker **Thomas P. O'Neill** (*see*) called the "finest speech" he had ever heard in Congress, the legislature approved an additional $200 million in aid to the Philippines. In addition to providing aid, the United States has acted to prevent Marcos' return to the Philippines, where he still hopes to regain power. Although Aquino squelched at least five coup attempts by military factions—Marcos loyalists—in her first eighteen months in office, she has achieved little success in negotiating a sustained cease-fire with the Communist insurgents. Despite the political unrest, Aquino has

instituted a number of economic reforms: breaking up sugar monopolies, reducing taxes, and, on March 3, 1987, introducing an ambitious land reform program designed to redistribute over 13 million acres of land to landless peasants and tenant farmers over the following five years. The Philippine government had eased some of the pressures on the economy by recovering over $400,000,000 in wealth corruptly amassed by Marcos during his rule, and within the next four months it would file seven suits in Manila courts seeking over $30 billion in theft, losses, and damages inflicted by Marcos during his tyranny. On February 2, 1987, Philippine voters overwhelmingly—by a margin of better that 5 to 1—backed the new constitution drafted by Aquino's committee. On May 11, the Philippine congressional elections seated 22 Aquino loyalists in the nation's 24-member Senate. When the new congress convened on July 27, Aquino declared an end to her transition government by decree and began her new constitutional duties as President. Although the Philippine political situation remains somewhat unstable, Aquino has vowed to complete her term—which expires in 1992—before retiring from political office.

B

THE BABY M. CASE. The Baby M. story began in February, 1985, when Mary Beth Whitehead, a New Jersey housewife and mother, signed a contract to bear a child for a couple named William and Elizabeth Stern. Because Elizabeth Stern, a pediatrician, was infertile, Mrs. Whitehead was to be artificially inseminated with Mr. Stern's sperm. If pregnancy resulted, Mrs. Whitehead was to hand over the baby at birth to the Sterns, relinquishing all her maternal rights. The Sterns, in turn, were to pay Whitehead a fee of $10,000. Mary Beth Whitehead was not the

Accompanied by a friend, Mary Beth Whitehead (right), Baby M.'s biological mother, visits her daughter in Hackensack, New Jersey in April, 1987.

first surrogate mother in America; dozens of women before her had given birth to babies for childless couples. But Mrs. Whitehead was unique in that when her baby girl was born on March 27, 1986, she changed her mind about giving up the child. Threatening suicide, she pleaded with the Sterns to give back her baby. When the Sterns temporarily complied, Whitehead kept the baby, ignoring a court order issued a month later that gave temporary custody of the infant to the Sterns. Having refused to accept any money at all from the Sterns, Whitehead and her husband fled with the baby to Florida. On July 31, 1986, detectives seized the four-month-old from the home of Mrs. Whitehead's mother, in Florida, and returned her to the Sterns. By now the baby, whom the Sterns had named Melissa and whom the Whiteheads had christened Sara, had become Baby M to vast numbers of the American public. Because there were no laws governing surrogate motherhood in New Jersey and most other states, people watched closely as the Sterns and the Whiteheads battled each other for permanent custody of the child through the state courts. Meanwhile, Baby M remained with the Sterns while her natural mother, Mary Beth Whitehead, retained visiting rights. In March, 1987, Judge

Harvey Sorkow of New Jersey's Superior Court stripped Mrs. Whitehead of all her parental rights, made Elizabeth Stern Melissa's legal mother, and granted permanent custody of the child to the Sterns. Whitehead next appealed to the State's highest court, the New Jersey Supreme Court. It ruled nearly a year later that the Sterns were the ones most suited to raise Melissa. But it restored Mary Beth Whitehead's maternal visitation rights. And most important of all, it said that it is illegal for women to become pregnant and give away their babies for money. According to Daniel Callahan of the Hastings Institute, a medical-ethics think-tank, "the ruling is going to seriously cast a chill over future surrogate contracts."

BAKER, Howard (born 1925). An influential Republican in the 1970s and 1980s, Baker became a stabilizing force in the White House as President **Ronald W. Reagan**'s (*see*) Chief of Staff following the **Iran-Contra scandal** (*see*). Baker was born into a powerful Tennessee family in 1925: his grandfather was a judge, his grandmother was the first woman sheriff in Tennessee, and his father served seven terms as a member of the U.S. House of Representatives. After graduating from a military academy in 1943,

Baker immediately enrolled in the Navy's officer training program, and he served as a lieutenant on a PT boat in the South Pacific during the final months of World War II. Returning to the United States, Baker enrolled at the University of Tennessee, where he received a bachelor's degree and a law degree. After gaining admission to the Tennessee bar in 1949, Baker joined the law firm his grandfather had founded, where he gained experience in criminal defense and corporate law. During the next fifteen years, while practicing law, Baker made highly profitable investments in banking and real estate, adding to the family fortune. In 1964, shortly after his father died and his stepmother finished her husband's term in the House of Representatives, Baker entered politics, running an unsuccessful, extremely conservative campaign to fill an unexpired Senate term. Two years later, he ran a more moderate campaign, endorsing fair-housing laws among other liberal legislation, and won 56% of the vote, becoming the first Republican Senator to win a Tennessee election. During three six-year terms as a Senator, Baker tended to vote conservatively on fiscal and defense issues, liberally on environmental issues and moderately or liberally on civil rights. While serving on the Committee on the Environment and Public Works, Baker sponsored anti-strip-mining legislation, the Clean Air Act of 1970, and the "Superfund" bill in 1980 that allocated funds for the cleanup of contaminated toxic waste dumps. On foreign-policy issues, he supported American military involvement in Southeast Asia and voted against the Salt II agreement. As the ranking Republican on the Senate committee investigating the Watergate scandal Baker gained national attention for his skilled cross-examination of witnesses. Although he favorably impressed the national public, he alienated many right-wing Republicans, who blamed him for adding to the pressure on President

Richard Nixon (born 1913) to resign. In 1976, hoping to win the vice presidential nomination, Baker delivered the keynote address at the Republican national convention, but Gerald R. Ford (born 1913) instead chose **Robert Dole** (*see*) as his running mate. In voting for ratification of the Panama Canal Treaty during President **Jimmy Carter**'s (*see*) administration, Baker further alienated the Republican Right, a split that may have cost him the Presidential or Vice-Presidential nomination in 1980. Despite the growing strength of the Republican Right, however, Baker had been elected Senate minority leader in 1977, and when the election victory of Ronald Reagan in 1980 led to Republican control of the Senate, Baker won election as the majority leader in 1981. In that capacity, he played a critical role in moving the President's tax proposals through the Senate and in building a consensus among the moderate and conservative wings of the Republican party. Baker retired from the Senate in 1984, returning to a private law practice that paid him well over $1,000,000 a year and gearing up for a possible 1988 Presidential campaign. After early 1987 polls showed him running third in his own party behind Vice President **George Bush** (*see*) and former Vice President **Robert Dole** (*see*), Baker sidelined his presidential aspirations, making himself available for other opportunities in government. Although he turned down an offer to replace the dying **William Casey** (*see*) as Director of Central Intelligence, Baker informed President Reagan that he would welcome the opportunity to serve on the Supreme Court or as Secretary of State. When, in the aftermath of the Iran-Contra hearings, the President accepted the resignation of White House Chief of Staff Donald Regan, he named Baker to succeed him. As Chief of Staff, Baker was credited with revitalizing morale and returning credibility to the administration. He immediately helped draft the speech in which the President explained to a national television audience his perspective on the Iran-Contra scandal. Baker advised against controversial Presidential nominations, persuading Reagan to nominate William Webster (born 1924), a former FBI director, as the new C.I.A. Chief, but he failed in two attempts to secure a Supreme Court nomination for Anthony Kennedy (born 1936), who ultimately became the President's choice after his first nominee, Robert Bork (born 1927), was rejected by the Senate and the second, Douglas Ginsburg (born 1946), withdrew because of the revelation that he had once smoked marijuana. In foreign policy, Baker advocated a tough stance in the Persian Gulf but urged President Reagan to respond favorably to Soviet leader **Mikhail Gorbachev**'s (*see*) arms-control overtures. A respected and effective Chief of Staff, Baker tended to delegate administrative responsibilities in the White House to his chief deputy, preferring—as he had throughout his career in the Senate—to devote himself to political strategy and policy making.

BELLOW, Saul (born 1915). One of the most acclaimed American authors of the twentieth century, Bellow received the Nobel Prize for Literature in 1976 for his fiction, which portrays contemporary characters facing alienation from society and struggling to preserve a sense of self in an increasingly complex world. Born in Montreal, Canada, Bellow moved to Chicago with his family in 1923. After graduating from high school in 1933, he entered the University of Chicago, but transferred to Northwestern University in 1935. He graduated from Northwestern in 1935 with a B.S. in anthropology and sociology. Bellow attended the University of Wisconsin at Madison for a time, but left the academic world to pursue a writing career, working with the New Deal's WPA writers' project and as an editor at *Encyclopedia Britan-* *nica*. During World War II, he served in the Merchant Marine. His first novel, *The Dangling Man,* was published in 1947. While teaching English at the University of Minnesota, Bellow received a Guggenheim Fellowship, which allowed him to move to Paris and complete another novel, *The Adventures of Augie March* (1953). It won the National Book Award. By the time his fifth book, *Henderson the Rain King,* appeared, in 1959, Bellow had achieved a reputation as a skilled literary craftsman and an astute observer of the human condition. *Herzog,* published in 1964, garnered Bellow a second National Book Award, and many readers and critics consider it his finest work. It was followed by *Mr. Sammler's Planet* in 1970, and *Humboldt's Gift* in 1975, which was awarded the Pulitzer Prize. Bellow's reputation as a great American writer was capped in 1976, when he became the sixth American to receive the Nobel Prize for Literature. Bellow, who now teaches at the Unversity of Chicago, has produced a body of work that includes not only novels but two plays and a collection of short stories.

BREZHNEV, Leonid Ilich (1906-1982). Leonid Brezhnev, whose tenure as leader of the Soviet Union spanned every presidency from John F. Kennedy (1917-1963) through **Ronald Reagan** (*see*), is a contradictory figure. He devoted great attention to promoting cooperation between the nations of eastern Europe and the Soviet Union, yet he sanctioned the ruthless suppression of liberal elements in Czechoslovakia in 1968; he sought a relaxation of tensions between the Soviet Union and the West, yet he presided over a vast buildup of Soviet military power and promoted movements aimed at toppling pro-western governments. Born in Kamenskoye, U.S.S.R., Brezhnev spent his early life as a land surveyor, engineer, and educational administrator. He joined the Communist Party in 1931, and during the reign of Josef Stalin (1879-1953), he rose quickly through the party's ranks. After war broke out between Germany and the Soviet Union, Brezhnev became a political officer in the Red Army. By 1943 he had attained the rank of major general and commanded all the political commissars on the vital Ukrainian front. After the war he continued with party work, eventually becoming a member of the Central Committee. After Stalin's death, Brezhnev lost his post on the Central Committee and served as Second Secretary of the Kazakhstan Communist Party; he also became a protege of Nikita Khrushchev (1894-1971). As a reward for his services to Khrushchev's agricultural programs, he regained his post on the Central Committee in 1956. Soon afterwards, he opposed an effort to oust Khrushchev from power, and in return for his loyalty he was made a member of the Presidium of the Soviet Union. In 1960, he became Chairman of the Presidium. He resigned that post in 1964 to work more closely with Khrushchev. Khrushchev's estimate of Brezhnev's loyalty proved false. In October, 1964, Brezhnev took part in the movement that toppled Khrushchev from power. Brezhnev shared power with Premier Aleksei Kosygin (1904-1980) for a short time, but it was soon apparent that Brezhnev would be the dominant figure. Brezhnev's chief goals were improved relations with the Soviet Union's satellite nations and the strengthening of Soviet military power. Authority for the Soviet Union's internal affairs and relations with western powers was left largely to his subordinates, Kosygin and Nikolai Podgorny (born 1903). Brezhnev's main domestic concern seemed to be the suppression of dissent within the Soviet Union and beyond its borders. The short-lived reform movement led by Alexander Dubcek (born 1921) in Czechoslovakia, was crushed by Warsaw Pact troops in the spring of 1968. Brezhnev pledged his support for what he called "wars of national liberation" in the Third World, and to that end the Soviet Union supplied arms and advisers to guerrilla movements around the globe. The Soviet Union gave arms to Arab nations in their struggle against Israel and to the North Vietnamese in their conflict with South Vietnam and the United States. In addition, arms, advisers, and technical assistance were provided to several African nations. Brezhnev's authority was strengthened by his reelection as General Secretary of the Communist Party in 1971. In 1976, he was given his country's highest military rank, Marshal of the Soviet Union, an honor previously claimed only by Stalin. In 1977, following the dismissal of Podgorny, Brezhnev became leader of both the Soviet Union and its Communist Party. Despite his rigid ideology and support for revolutionary movements, Brezhnev sought improved relations between the Soviet Union and the West. As part of this policy of detente, Brezhnev met with President Richard Nixon (born 1913) in Moscow in May, 1972. The two leaders reached agreements on a number of issues, including the Strategic Arms Limitation Talks (SALT) aimed at slowing the arms race. A summit in 1979 with President Jimmy Carter (born 1924) in Geneva proved less successful when Congress failed to ratify the SALT II treaty. Partly in response to western criticism of human rights in the Soviet Union, Brezhnev eased restrictions against the emigration of Soviet Jews and dissidents in the late 1970s. In poor health for much of the 1970s, Brezhnev died of a heart attack on November 10, 1982. He was succeeded by former KGB head Yuri Andropov (1914-1984).

BUSH, George Herbert Walker (born 1924). Twice elected Vice President on the Republican ticket with President **Ronald Reagan**

George Bush

(*see*), George Bush was a leading candidate for the Republican nomination for President in 1988. Few officials in modern times have served in the federal government in as many important roles or under as many Presidents. Bush was born in Milton, Massachusetts, on June 12, 1924. His father was Prescott Bush (1895-1972), a banker who for a decade was a Republican Senator from Connecticut. After schooling at Phillips Academy at Andover, Massachusetts, Bush served during World War II as a Navy carrier pilot. He was awarded the Distinguished Flying Cross and three Air Medals for combat missions in the Pacific. In 1945 he married Barbara Pierce; they have had six children, the second of whom died as a child. Bush graduated from Yale in 1946, earning a degree in economics in only two and a half years, along with Phi Beta Kappa honors. The Bushes then moved to Texas, where George began his business career as a salesman in the oil industry. In 1953, with two partners, he founded the Zapata Petroleum Corporation, and, in 1954, its offshoot, the Zapata Off Shore Company. He ran for the U.S. Senate from Texas in 1960 but was defeated. In 1966, he was elected to the U.S. House of Representatives from Texas's Seventh District, which includes Houston. His conservative voting record won him reelection in 1968. He ran for the Senate a second time in 1970, but was defeated once again. In 1971 President Richard Nixon (born 1913) appointed Bush U.S. Ambassador to the United Nations, a post he held for two years. A rapid succession of major appointments then followed: chairman of the Republican National Committee in 1973; head of the U.S. mission to mainland China, 1974; Director of Central Intelligence, 1976. In 1978 he returned to business in Texas, and a year later he announced his candidacy for the Republican nomination for President. Bush won a number of early caucuses and primaries in 1980, but by May he trailed **Ronald Reagan** (*see*) in delegates, bowed out of the race, and asked his delegates to support Reagan. In July, 1980, Reagan asked the Republican National Committee to name Bush as his running mate. In November, 1980, the Reagan-Bush ticket easily defeated the Democratic nominees, President **Jimmy Carter** (*see*) and Vice President **Walter Mondale** (*see*). An even more lopsided victory was won by Reagan and Bush in 1984 over Democrats Mondale and **Geraldine Ferraro** (*see*). As Vice President, George Bush became one of President Reagan's inner circle of advisers, especially in foreign affairs and national security matters. He traveled to many foreign countries as the President's emissary and spokesman. Among other special assignments given him were jobs as head of a cabinet-level task force on reform of federal regulatory agencies, and as coordinator of federal programs to combat drug smuggling. For a few hours in July, 1985, while President Reagan was undergoing surgery, Bush was Acting President under Article XXV of the Constitution.

C

CARTER, Jimmy (James Earl, Jr.) (born 1924). Jimmy Carter's election as President in November, 1976, capped a remarkable rise from obscurity to national fame. In late December, 1974, ineligible to seek reelection as Governor of Georgia and little known elsewhere, Carter had begun to work intensively to win the 1976 Democratic nomination for President. His chief rivals were Senator Henry M. Jackson (1912-1983), Representative Morris K. Udall (born 1922), and Alabama Governor George C. Wallace (born 1919). In January, 1976, Carter won the Iowa caucus and followed this with stunning victories in the New Hampshire and Florida primaries. Altogether, he captured the delegates in 18 primaries and won the Democratic nomination on the first ballot. He chose as his Vice-Presidential running mate Senator **Walter F. Mondale** (*see*) of Minnesota. In the ensuing campaign against the Republican incumbent, Gerald R. Ford (born 1913), Carter made much of the public's disillusionment over the Watergate affair and President Ford's subsequent blanket pardon of Richard M. Nixon (born 1913). The Carter candidacy offered the prospect of a leader not associated with Washington and its doings, who had no ties to special interests, and who would restore respect for the office of President. On election day Jimmy Carter defeated President Ford in a close race, 297 electoral votes to 240. The first native of Georgia to be elected President, Carter was born in Plains, Georgia, on October 1, 1924, the son of James Earl Carter (1894-1953) and Lillian Gordy Carter (1898-1983). His father was a farmer, and as a boy, Jimmy sold his father's peanuts on the streets of Plains. Carter entered Georgia Southwestern College, in Americus, Georgia, in 1941. In 1942 he received an appointment to the U.S. Naval Academy, but lacking credentials in mathematics, he first enrolled at Georgia Institute of Technology and then entered the Naval Academy in 1943. At graduation in 1946 he ranked 59th in a class of 820 midshipmen. On July 7, 1946, he married Rosalynn Smith (born 1927), also of Plains. The Carters would later have four children. Carter served in the Navy until 1953, first as an electronics engineering officer on the battleships U.S.S. *Wyoming* and *Mississippi*. In 1948 he volunteered for submarine duty. His training in submarine operations and anti-submarine warfare from 1948 to 1951 led to his assignment in 1952 to a group of officers chosen to help develop the world's first nuclear-powered submarine, the U.S.S. *Nautilus,* which was launched in 1954. In this program he came under the tutelage of Captain (later Admiral) Hyman G. Rickover (1906-1986). When Carter's father died, in 1953, he resigned his commission and returned to Plains to manage the family business, expanding it into cotton ginning and fertilizer sales. Carter was elected to the Sumter County Board of Education in 1955 and was active in regional-development organizations and the Plains Baptist Church. Known as a fiscal conservative but social liberal, Carter ran for the Georgia Senate in 1962. In the Democratic primary the close vote went against him, but the irregularities permitted by an election supervisor had been so blatant that Carter was declared the winner. He defeated his Republican opponent easily; he was reelected in 1964. Carter tried for the Democratic nomination for Governor of Georgia in 1966, but lost. He ran again in 1970, making 1,800 speeches across the state on Georgia's problems and their solutions. His strategy won the party's nomination and the subsequent general election. His four-year term was marked by a restructuring of the state government, the enactment of environmental-protection legislation, merit appointment of judges and state officials, and the opening of many job opportunities for blacks. Directly after his inauguration as President, Carter fulfilled his cam-

Jimmy and Rosalyn Carter

paign pledge to pardon Vietnam War draft evaders. In March, 1981, Congress approved his plan to consolidate the operations of government agencies which duplicated one another's services—another campaign pledge. A promise to develop a strategy to cope with energy problems led to the creation of the Energy Department. In an attempt to trim the military budget, Carter halted the production of the B-1 bomber in favor of the more flexible, less expensive cruise missile. By 1978 inflation had become a major problem once again. A major cause of this was the manipulation of oil prices by the Organization of Petroleum Exporting Countries (OPEC), dominated by Middle Eastern interests. In 1979 gasoline shortages deepened and inflation worsened. Carter's earlier successes in foreign policy, especially the remarkable Camp David accord in 1978 that brought an agreement between Egypt's Anwar el-Sadat (1918-1981) and Israel's Menachem Begin (born 1913), could not stop Carter's fall in approval ratings to a low of 21% in July, 1980. Other Carter achievements in foreign policy include the

Panama Canal treaty, which was ratified by the Senate in 1978, and negotiations with the Soviet Union to limit the use of nuclear weapons. The resulting Strategic Arms Limitation Treaty, or SALT II, failed to be ratified by the Senate in the wake of the Soviet invasion of Afghanistan. Capping Carter's problems was the seizure in November, 1979, of the U.S. Embassy in Teheran, Iran, and all its American personnel, by Moslem followers of the Ayatollah Ruhollah Khomeini (born 1900?). The hostage taking was Khomeini's response to the admission of Shah Mohammed Reza Pahlevi (1920-1980) into the United States for medical treatment. Carter banned all imports from Iran, terminated diplomatic relations, and froze Iranian assets in the United States. In April, 1980, he approved an armed mission to rescue the hostages, but it failed when three of the eight helicopters malfunctioned and another collided with a transport plane, killing eight and injuring five. Though the Shah died in July, 1980, the Ayatollah's hatred did not. He finally released the hostages the day after Carter left office. Carter had been renominated by the Democrats in the summer of 1980, but with the handicaps of inflation and the unreturned hostages, he was badly defeated by the Republican nominee, **Ronald Reagan** (*see*), 489 electoral votes to 49.

CASEY, William Joseph (1913-1987). A crafty spy during World War II, a venture capitalist who made millions in investments for himself and then made it harder for others by regulating stock trades as chairman of the Securities and Exchange Commission (S.E.C.), but above all a gruff spymaster who directed the Central Intelligence Agency (C.I.A.) for six years, Casey died just one day after the first witness appeared before the joint Congressional committee investigating the **Iran-Contra Affair** (*see*). As the committee readily acknowl-

edged when it released its findings, the death of Casey left "the record incomplete," for he was probably better informed about the covert operation than anyone else except Lieutenant Colonel Oliver North (born 1943), the National Security council (N.S.C.) staff member in charge of the enterprise. Born in Queens, New York, Casey graduated from Fordham University in 1934 and received his law degree from St. John's University three years later. He then joined the Research Institute of America, which analyzed information and made economic and political predictions based on the effects of President Franklin D. Roosevelt's (1882-1945) New Deal legislation. Throughout World War II, Casey served with Army Intelligence and the Office of Strategic Services—the predecessor to the C.I.A.—running spies behind German lines from a base in London, where he shared an apartment with colleague and future C.I.A. head Richard M. Helms (born 1913). From 1948 to 1962, he lectured on tax law at New York University, and in 1957, he became a partner in a New York law firm. In 1964, he failed in his attempt to win the Republican nomination for a Congressional seat, but four years later he campaigned, researched, and wrote for Richard M. Nixon (born 1913) in his successful Presidential bid. After establishing a lobbying organization that supported Nixon's anti-ballistic-missile programs and serving on the advisory council of the Arms Control and Disarmament Agency, Casey left his law practice in 1971, when the President nominated him to be chairman of the S.E.C. There, he imposed strict policies designed to improve regulation of the issuance and trading of stocks. In 1973, Secretary of State William P. Rogers (born 1913) named Casey as his Undersecretary for Economic Affairs, a post he held until 1974, when Henry A. Kissinger (born 1923) succeeded Rogers. Casey next headed the Export-

Import Bank, an independent agency that facilitates the export of American goods and services, and served on President Gerald R. Ford's (born 1913) Foreign Intelligence Advisory Board. In 1976, he returned to the private sector, becoming affiliated with Rogers's law firm. But in 1979, after turning down requests for support from John B. Connally (born 1917) and **George Bush** (*see*), Casey lent his political backing to **Ronald Reagan** (*see*), and agreed to run Reagan's 1980 Presidential campaign. When the Reagan-Bush team won the election that November, the President-elect nominated Casey—who shared his vision of the Soviet Union as an "evil empire"—as Director of Central Intelligence. A trusted adviser to the President, Casey became the first C.I.A. Director to act as a fully participating Cabinet member. During the first three fiscal years of the Reagan administration, Casey increased the intelligence budget by 50% and directed hundreds of millions of dollars to anti-Communist guerillas in developing countries throughout the world: **Nicaragua** (*see*), Afghanistan, Angola, Ethiopia, and Cambodia. As the Congressional Iran-Contra Committee later concluded, Casey had a "passion for covert operations," a passion he demonstrated throughout his tenure as CIA chief. Under his leadership, the agency provided military assistance and clandestine instruction to Contra troops in Nicaragua, secretly mined Nicaraguan harbors, and compiled a training manual that advised contras on directing "selective use of violence" against civilian officials. In addition to his efforts to topple the government of Nicaragua, Casey recruited over two dozen spies living within the Soviet Union, and—according to Washington Post reporter Bob Woodward in his book *Veil: The Secret Wars of the CIA 1981-1987*—orchestrated an attempt to assassinate Lebanon's Shiite leader Sheik Mohammed Hussein Fadlallah. The March 8, 1985, car

bombing failed to kill Fadlallah, but cost 80 innocent people their lives. Although Casey improved the C.I.A.'s analytical capabilities and modernized its methods of intelligence gathering, his secrecy and dubious methods caused many critics to call for his resignation even before the events of the Iran-Contra scandal began to unfold. On December 15, 1986, one day before he was scheduled to appear before a Senate panel to explain the C.I.A.'s role in the arms sale to Iran, Casey was hospitalized for surgical removal of a malignant brain tumor. He resigned his C.I.A. post on February 2, 1987, and died of pneumonia on May 7, one day after retired Air Force officer Richard V. Secord (born 1932) testified that Casey had assisted him in illegally providing arms to the Nicaraguan rebels. In November, 1987, when the Congressional Committee issued its findings, it charged that Casey had known of the diversion of profits from the Iran arms sales to the Nicaragua rebels, although it conceded that only Oliver North had testified to this fact (Woodward's book also claims Casey admitted this knowledge). The report criticized Casey harshly for subverting democratic processes—by sponsoring an "off-the-shelf, self-sustaining" covert operations network that would avoid Congressional scrutiny and by misrepresenting and selectively using intelligence data to influence administration decisions.

THE CHALLENGER DISASTER. On January 28, 1986, 73 seconds after liftoff and nine miles above the Atlantic ocean, the Space Shuttle *Challenger* exploded, as millions of horrified Americans—including schoolchildren in their classes—watched on television. The *Challenger* launch was to have begun the nation's twenty-fifth space-shuttle mission. A nation prepared for celebration went into mourning. Aboard the shuttle had been Gregory Jarvis (1944-1986); Ronald McNair

(1950-1986)—the second black American astronaut; Ellison Onizuka (1946-1986); Judith Resnick (1949-1986)—the second American woman astronaut; Francis Scobee (1939-1986); Michael Smith (1945-1986); and Christa McAuliffe (1948-1986), of Concord, New Hampshire. McAuliffe, a schoolteacher, had been selected to be the first American civilian in space, and she had been going to broadcast lessons about space from aboard the shuttle. The shock of the *Challenger* tragedy was felt especially by the thousands of children who awaited the first lessons from space. In addition to McAuliffe's lessons, the *Challenger's* crew was planning to measure the ultraviolet spectrum of Halley's comet and sample radiation at different points within the spacecraft. In an effort to understand the precise cause of the catastrophe, divers and salvage teams scoured the waters off Cape Kennedy for any scrap of debris which might give investigators a clue. Within a few days, the main mechanical problem was pinpointed: An O-ring seal, a kind of gasket at a joint on one of the rocket boosters that were to propel the *Challenger* into space, had failed. It was discovered that shuttle technicians were aware of the flaw, but this knowledge had become buried in paperwork as the management of the National Aeronautics and Space Administration (N.A.S.A.) pushed to keep the launch—already postponed once due to poor weather—on schedule. The *Challenger* tragedy was a costly setback to the American manned space program. All further shuttle launches were postponed until investigators could be completely satisfied that the errors that sent the *Challenger* down were completely resolved. The extensive investigation resulted in recommendations for stricter safety procedures, greater accountability on the part of N.A.S.A.and its contractors, and the participation of astronauts themselves in spacecraft design.

D

AMERICAN TELEPHONE & TELEGRAPH COMPANY

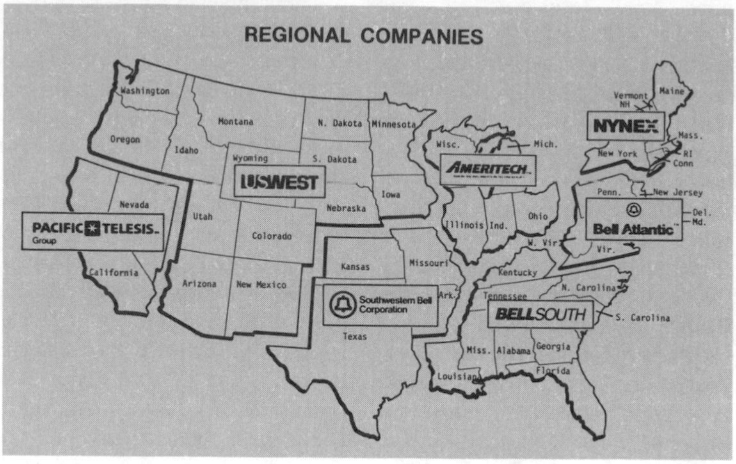

This map shows the different regional companies created by the breakup of A.T.&T.

DEREGULATION OF INDUSTRY. As part of the "New Federalism," **Ronald Reagan** (*see*) pledged, during his successful bid for the presidency in 1980, to ease or eliminate much of the federal regulation of private industry that had grown up since the beginning of the twentieth century, and particularly since 1960. The 1960 *Federal Register*, which lists all proposed and final federal regulations, had 9,562 pages. By 1980, the *Register* had grown to 87,012 pages. According to Reagan, his cabinet, and much of Congress, business was struggling under the weight of federal rules which, they believed, inhibited growth, shortchanged the consumer, and contributed to the ever-increasing federal deficit. Reagan stated that in the absence of federal regulation, the "magic of the marketplace"—competition—would provide consumers with the best products and services at the lowest possible costs. The trend towards deregulation had begun not with Reagan but with President **Jimmy Carter** (*see*). In 1978, Congress passed the Airline Deregulation Act, which removed federal restrictions on passenger fares and other aspects of the airline industry. Airline deregulation was intended to spur competition, increase air service, and lower the cost of airline travel. Airline fares did decline by 13% in 1986, but the six largest carriers benefited, winning 84% of the business, as the lower prices forced many smaller carriers into mergers or bankruptcy. Also, a spate of fatal commercial plane crashes led some Americans to believe deregulation had decreased the safety of air travel along with its cost. Deregulation of other parts of the transportation industry, especially trucking and the railroads, began in 1980, and between 1980 and 1985 the percentage of the Gross National Product spent on shipping goods dropped from 8.1% to 7.3%—a significant reduction in the nation's freight bill. Without the protection afforded by federal regulation, however, many smaller trucking firms were forced to merge with larger carriers or go out of business altogether. Critics of transportation deregulation charged that instead of encouraging business, deregulation actually made it extremely difficult for small, independent carriers to enter the industry. Another area to undergo deregulation was banking. Individual states had begun to deregulate banking in the 1960s and 1970s, and this trend expanded in 1980 when the federal government removed limits on interest rates. Banks began to extend their operations beyond their traditional roles as savings institutions, and beyond their strictly defined geographical limits. Many smaller banks were absorbed by larger financial institutions, and the competition increased the number of bank failures. A number of banking institutions entered financial markets such as securities, creating new competition for traditional stockbrokers and mutual funds. Perhaps the most notable single act of deregulation was the restructuring of the monolithic American Telephone & Telegraph Company, which for decades had dominated American long-distance communications, despite repeated charges of monopolism and restraint of trade. While the breakup of A.T.&T. was actually an instance of regulation by the federal government, its intent was in keeping with the philosophy of deregulation—the decreased influence of A.T.&T., it was hoped, would spur competition and encourage lower rates in the communications industry. In 1984, A.T.& T. was split up, and its transmission operations taken over by a number of smaller, regional companies which, in turn, met with competition, in rates and services, from other companies, including General Telephone and Electronics Corporation. American businesses and individuals were given the opportunity to choose long-distance companies, and a large percentage chose to stay with A.T.&T., making it difficult for the newer companies to establish themselves in the market. Communications costs have dropped for businesses, but the advantage of this has been offset, in many cases, by increased paperwork and the complications of choosing a new telephone system. Deregulation has had a broad and mixed effect on the lives of individuals—everyone likes the lower prices a purer free-market economy encourages, but the side effects can be troublesome.

DOLE, Elizabeth Hanford (born 1936). As the first woman to head the U.S. Department of Transportation, Elizabeth Dole became the first woman in American history to have executive control over a branch of the armed forces—the Coast Guard. Now considered a moderate Republican, Dole spent ten years as a Democrat working for the Johnson administration, and also several years as registered Independent in the early 1970s. She was born Elizabeth Hanford on July 20, 1936, in Salisbury, North Carolina, to a prosperous family involved in the wholesale flower business. She graduated from Duke University in 1958, earned a Master's in Education from Harvard in 1960, and then enrolled in Harvard Law School as one of 15 women in a starting class of 550. While working for the Assistant Secretary of the Department of Health, Education, and Welfare in the mid-1960s, she organized the first national conference on education for the deaf. In 1968, she moved into consumer affairs, becoming an Associate Director for President Lyndon Johnson's (1908-1972) Commission on Consumer Interests, a position which would carry her into the Nixon era. Her work in this area led her to meet a Republican Senator from Kansas, **Robert Dole** (*see*). The two were married in 1975. Appointed by Nixon in 1973 to the five-member Federal Trade Commission, Elizabeth Dole served for six years promoting competition in American industry. In 1979, She resigned her F.T.C. post to support her husband in his short fight for the Republican presidential nomination. When President **Ronald Reagan** (*see*) took office in 1981, he appointed Mrs. Dole to the position of Assistant to the President for Public Liaison, a key White House position. Women's organizations criticized Dole for her apparent abandonment of the Equal Rights Amendment, which she had previously supported. Reagan made her a member of the Cabinet as Secretary of Tranportation in 1983. Making safety her number one priority, Dole

Elizabeth Dole

Robert Dole

worked to improve air-traffic safety and compel states to raise the drinking age to 21. She instituted a plan to promote women in the Department, redirected billions of dollars of contracts to minority-owned businesses, and deregulated many industries. In 1987, Dole resigned her post to help her husband in his bid for the 1988 Republican Presidential nomination. She had had the longest tenure of any Secretary of Transportation.

DOLE, Robert Joseph (born 1923). Robert Dole was the Republican party's nominee for Vice President in 1976. He has served as Senate Republican leader, and has been a member of such influential Senate committees as the Senate Finance Committee and the Senate Rules Committee. Dole was born in Russell, Kansas, in 1923. He attended the University of Kansas, studying medicine, and enlisted in the Army during World War II. In 1945, while serving as a platoon leader in Italy, he was seriously wounded by an exploding shell. He spent 39 months in hospitals recovering from his wounds, and lost the use of his right arm. He received a Bronze Star with cluster for his bravery in action. Dole graduated from Washburn University, in Topeka, Kansas, in 1952 and shortly thereafter completed the requirements for a

law degree at the same institution. In 1950, while still a student, he won election to the Kansas House of Representatives. In 1952, he was elected County attorney, and he was reelected to both offices several times. In 1960, he was elected to the U.S. House of Representatives from Kansas, and he won three successive reelections. In 1968, he ran successfully for the U.S. Senate. He served as chairman of the Republican National Committee from 1970 to 1973. Unblemished by the Watergate scandal, he was reelected Senator in 1974, emerging as one of the most influential figures on Capitol Hill. Generally conservative, especially in fiscal matters, Dole was a partisan defender of President Nixon's controversial Supreme Court nominations and the President's actions in Southeast Asia. His voting record was by no means rigidly conservative: he voted for most civil-rights programs, the food-stamp program, and aid for the handicapped, and he has steadfastly supported the agricultural interests of his home-state constituents. On the campaign trail and in Senate debates, Dole is known for his party loyalty, quick wit, and often sarcastic criticism of opposition; he has also been called a realist, a negotiator, and a politician capable of achieving compromise and consensus. Dole's first marriage ended in divorce. His second marriage, on December 6, 1975, was to Elizabeth Hanford, at the time a member of the Federal Trade Commission. She resigned that post in 1979 to campaign for Robert Dole in the 1980 Presidential race. Dole's years of service to his party and nation made him a leading early contender for the Republican Presidential nomination in 1988.

E

EQUAL RIGHTS AMENDMENT (E.R.A.).

The Equal Rights Amendment was proposed in order to make discrimination on the basis of gender a direct violation of the U.S. Constitution, but it never gained enough support in individual state legislatures to achieve ratification. Had it passed into law, the E.R.A. would have been the Twenty-Seventh Amendment to the Constitution. First drafted in 1923 and presented to Congress by the National Women's Party, the text of the amendment reads: "Equality of rights under the law shall not be denied or abridged by the United States or any state on account of sex." In 1970, the National Organization for Women (N.O.W.) initiated a campaign in support of the proposed amendment. The E.R.A. passed in the House in 1971 and in the Senate the following year; all that remained before it could become law was for 38 states to ratify it within seven years. In the year following the E.R.A.'s passage in Congress, it was ratified by the legislatures of 30 states. However, due in part to the lobbying activities of anti-E.R.A. groups, three states rescinded their ratifications, and the proposed amendment was ratified by only three more states. In 1978, Congress voted to extend the ratification period to 1982. In 1980, the Republican party dropped support for the E.R.A. from its platform. When the deadline for ratification came, only 35 states had approved the proposed amendment; last-minute efforts by E.R.A. advocates to sway the legislatures of the states that had voted down the E.R.A. proved unsuccessful. An attempt in 1983 to reintroduce the E.R.A. in Congress was also unsuccessful, despite polls indicating that most Americans approved of the proposed amendment. Opponents of the E.R.A. argued that it was redundant, since equal protection under the law is guaranteed to all Americans, regardless of sex, under the Fourteenth Amendment. Others contended that inequality was a fact of biology rather than politics, and that passage of the E.R.A. would undermine social institutions such as the family and the home.

F

FARM FAILURES.

Since the early 1980s, one rural image has become all too familiar on the nightly news: An auctioneer, standing on the back of a pickup truck, is selling farm equipment on behalf of a bank to defray part of the debt of yet another failed small or medium-sized family farm. We see the bankrupt farmer and his family, tears in their eyes, watching their way of life disappear. Between June, 1981, and June, 1987, the number of farms in America declined by more than 260,000, to a low of 2.7 million. In Nebraska and Iowa alone, almost a third of all farm-equipment dealers have gone out of business since 1986. According to experts, the crisis has resulted largely from an overexpansion of farm production in the 1970s, when exports soared and retail food prices rose. Farmers borrowed heavily to expand their acreage and purchase new farm machinery. Many went

In September, 1985, a number of popular rock and country musicians banded together for a "Farm Aid" concert to raise money to help farmers in danger of losing their land.

deeply into debt. Then, in the 1980s, foreign demand fell and domestic prices for agricultural products dropped sharply. Farmers found themselves in a losing struggle to pay heavy interest costs. The farm recession continued into 1988, although at a slower rate—approximately 10% of all farmers still suffer from excessive debt and low income, according to the United States Department of Agriculture. By the end of 1987, some encouraging signs had begun to appear. That year set a record for net cash income for farmers—the money they have left over to pay living expenses and long-term debts after paying other expenses. However, one of the long-range problems facing American agriculture is that not all farmers share in the profits. The biggest 1.3% of American farms—those with gross sales of $300,000 or more—bring in close to 50% of all farm profits and receive 9% of government agricultural subsidies, which cost U.S. taxpayers $49 billion in 1986 and 1987. In early 1988, new regulations were announced by the Farmer's Home Administration, a division of the Department of Agriculture intended to relieve small and medium-acreage farmers of some of their $7 billion in collective debt by restructuring payment terms, helping some 100,000 hard-pressed farmers keep their land. But the regulations were not universally accepted within the Department of Agriculture. Some felt that the relaxation of credit terms would not have beneficial long-term effects. "As a farmer, I'm unhappy about it," said Oscar Brand, a farmer and director of the Farmer's Home Administration in Indiana. "We already have huge farm surpluses, yet here we are keeping farmers producing. We may have too many farmers in this country."

FERRARO, Geraldine A. (born 1935). Although the Democratic Mondale-Ferraro ticket lost the 1984 presidential election by a wide margin, Ferraro—the first woman ever

nominated for the vice presidency by a major party—fulfilled the dreams of millions of American women who saw her as a symbol of victory in the struggle for sexual equality. Born in 1935, Ferraro was the only daughter of an Italian immigrant who had become a successful restaurateur and store owner in Newburgh, New York. She suffered a great loss when her father died when she was just seven years old. The Ferraro family then moved to the Bronx, where her mother saved just enough money to send her to Catholic girls' schools. Winning a scholarship to Marymount College, Ferraro majored in English and received her B.A. degree in 1956. After that, she took night classes at Fordham University Law School while teaching in Queens public schools during the day. In 1960 she earned her law degree and married John Zaccaro, a lawyer, but continued to use her maiden name professionally. Following her admission to the New York State Bar, in 1961, Ferraro chose to devote herself to raising a family while working part-time as a civil lawyer, often in connection with her husband's real-estate business. She channeled her political energies into campaigning and volunteer work in behalf of local Democratic candidates. In 1974, Ferraro was appointed an assistant district attorney in Queens, her first full-time job as a lawyer. In 1975, she helped create a Special Victims Bureau in the district attorney's office, to investigate and prosecute cases involving domestic violence, child abuse, and rape. She worked in the bureau for four years, two of them as its head, and acquired a reputation for toughness, fairness, persuasiveness, and professionalism as a prosecutor. Her work with victims and her growing conviction that poverty and social injustice lay at the root of many of these crimes transformed her political philosophy from moderate conservatism to dedicated liberalism. In 1978 she resigned from the District Attorney's

office to enter the political arena, running for U.S. Congress on a campaign espousing support for the elderly, neighborhood preservation, and law and order—issues important in her largely working-class congressional district. Ferraro won election by a ten-point margin, a success she would duplicate in re-election campaigns in 1980 and 1982. While in Congress, Ferraro usually voted the liberal, pro-labor Democratic party line: strongly advocating women's rights issues, aid to Israel, and a verifiable nuclear freeze, while opposing reductions in funds for social programs and the deployment of the MX missile system. Her major departure from Democratic voting patterns came on issues of defense spending: An advocate of a strong defense, Ferraro supported funding for the Pershing II nuclear missile and the Trident nuclear submarine. She also opposed mandatory busing. In 1984, a year after winning an appointment to the Budget Committee, her first major committee assignment, Ferraro chaired the Democratic platform committee, a highly influential post within the party. Her success at forging a broad thematic document favorable to the vast majority of party members positioned her as a front-runner in the race to secure Democratic presidential candidate **Walter F. Mondale**'s (*see*) nomination as his running mate. Mondale—anticipating not only the media exposure generated by the nomination of a woman as a candidate for the vice presidency, but also counting on Ferraro to win the votes of women, voters from industrial states in the northeast, Italian Americans, and Roman Catholics—announced his selection of Ferraro as his running mate on July 12, 1984. No sooner had they begun their campaign than Ferraro came under fire for her reluctance to release her husband's tax returns. Later it was disclosed that she had owed over $50,000 in back taxes and interest. In August, Ferraro handled a grueling two-hour press con-

Geraldine Ferraro

ference with coolness and confidence, emerging with her reputation, dignity, and integrity intact. Ferraro impressed most political observers during the campaign, especially in a nationally televised vice-presidential debate against **George Bush** (*see*), but her efforts did not win over the electorate, as the Mondale-Ferraro ticket won electoral votes only from Minnesota and the District of Columbia. Although the campaign had failed, Ferraro's nomination, concretely demonstrating the gains achieved by the century-long women's rights movement, was seen by many as a victory in itself.

G

GORBACHEV, Mikhail Sergeyevich (born 1931). Mikhail Gorbachev, Secretary General of the Communist Party of the Soviet Union since March, 1985, was born in the village of Privonoye in the southern region of the Russian Republic of the U.S.S.R., not far from Stavropol. Gorbachev began his political career as a youth, in the *Komsomol,* the youth training league for future Communist Party members. He became one of the league's organizers at the University of Moscow in 1952. In 1954, Gorbachev married Raisa Maximovna Titorenko, a philosophy student at the

University of Moscow. He graduated with a law degree in 1955. There is little public information regarding Gorbachev for the next 23 years, except that he returned to Stavropol and evidently rose through the ranks of the Communist Party there. He also continued his studies during these years and received a degree in agriculture from the Stavropol Agricultural Institute in 1967. In 1978, Gorbachev was appointed Communist Party Central Committee Secretary in charge of agriculture, a position that ranked him 20th in the Soviet hierarchy. At age 49, he was made a full member of the Politburo—21 years younger than the average age of the other members. A visit to Canada in 1983 convinced him that the Soviet Union was a half-century behind the West in agriculture, and desperately in need of reform. In March, 1985, at age 54, Gorbachev became General Secretary of the Communist Party, a position that carried with it the leadership of the Soviet Union. The youngest General Secretary in the Soviet Union's history, he brought the party and the nation new energy and hope for the future. He was an advocate of *Perestroika*—restructuring—of the Soviet Union's economic system, including legalization (although on a small scale) of some private enterprise. He also proclaimed *Glasnost,* a new openness, including increased tolerance for opposing viewpoints. Some steps were taken to correct blatant human rights violations, including a partial relaxation of the laws prohibiting the emigration of Soviet Jews and dissidents. He also began an avid campaign against the widespread alcoholism that saps the nation's productivity. The world, particularly the democratic nations of the West, closely examined Gorbachev's reforms, hoping that the new openness would lead to peace and a lessening of tension between East and West. Gorbachev seemed sincere, if only because he seemed to fully realize that peace and improved foreign re-

lations were necessary for the restructuring of the ailing Soviet economy. In December, 1987, General Secretary Gorbachev signed a treaty with President **Ronald Reagan** (*see*), providing for the removal of large numbers of intermediate-range nuclear missiles from Europe.

GRENADA. On the night of October 24, 1983, President Reagan called House Speaker **Thomas P. "Tip" O'Neill, Jr.** (*see*) and the majority and minority leaders of the Senate and House of Representatives to the White House, and quietly informed them that the United States and several Caribbean nations were about to undertake a military invasion of the troubled island nation of Grenada. Grenada, in the southern Caribbean Sea, is about 130 square miles in size and has a population of approximately 88,000. Formerly a British colony, Grenada gained its independence within the British Commonwealth in 1974, becoming the smallest independent nation in the Western Hemisphere. The government of Grenada's first Prime Minister, Sir Eric M. Gairy, was overthrown in a military coup on March 13, 1979. The coup had been engineered by Maurice Bishop, leader of the Marxist "New Jewel" movement ("Joint Endeavor for Welfare, Education, and Liberation"). Bishop, an admirer of Cuban President Fidel Castro (born 1927), invited Soviet and Cuban technicians, advisers, and workers to Grenada. One of their projects was the construction of a new airport, with a 12,000-foot airstrip on the island's southern tip. Large quantities of Russian and Cuban weapons were stockpiled on the island. Bishop exhorted his followers to fight "a people's war" against imperialism. In early October, 1983, Bishop was killed in a military coup and replaced by Hudson Austin, an even more fervent Marxist. The leaders of other Caribbean nations looked on the unrest in Grenada, and its increasing ties with Cuba and the Soviet Union, with mounting anxiety. Five member nations of the Organization of Eastern Caribbean States formally requested the United States to intervene in force to restore order. Many U.S. leaders were concerned about the situation in Grenada, and the Reagan administration was eager to cut short the rise of a new Marxist-dominated government in the Western Hemisphere. And there was another factor behind American military intervention. About 1,100 American citizens, most of them medical students, were in Grenada. They were in no immediate danger, but the possibility of another drawn-out hostage crisis like the one in Iran had to be considered. The President decided to launch an invasion to Grenada in order to reduce the "threat to the peace and security of that region." On October 24, 1983, Operation "Urgent Fury" began. That night, teams of U.S. Navy SEAL commandos secretly landed at key points on the island's coast. In the early morning of the 25th, U.S. Marines landed by helicopter to take control of Pearls Airport. An hour later, U.S. Army Rangers parachuted onto the unfinished airstrip at Point Salines. Another Marine force landed near the capital city of St. George's. Elements of the Army's 82nd Airborne Division and a multinational force from Barbados, Dominica, Jamaica, St. Lucia, and St. Vincent were also flown in. In all, some 1,900 American and Caribbean troops took part in the operation. The invading forces quickly gained control in most areas, although the Rangers encountered fierce resistance from the Cubans at Point Salines. Fighting in St. George's ended on October 27th, and within three days Hudson Austin was captured and resistance ended. Most Grenadians welcomed the American troops warmly. The medical students and other Americans were evacuated to the United States. Eighteen Americans were killed and 116 wounded; Grenadian casualties totalled 45 killed and 337 wounded,

and Cuban casualties were 24 killed and 59 wounded. The Grenada operation was a success, although admittedly a small one. It restored a measure of pride to the American military establishment, which was still smarting from the deaths of 241 Marines in a terrorist bombing in Beirut only a few days before. While most Americans seemed to support President Reagan's decision to invade Grenada, some charged that it marked a return to "gunboat diplomacy" and the days when the United States imposed its will on the Caribbean by military force. These critics argued that the United States had no right to intervene in a sovereign nation's internal affairs on such a scale, and that the official justification for the operation—as a rescue mission to protect American citizens—was just a flimsy pretext for ousting a Marxist presence from the Caribbean. The operation was also criticized in the news media after military authorities prohibited news crews from covering the combat phase of the invasion. Also, it was charged that the President had overstepped the bounds of executive authority in ordering the invasion and had very nearly violated the War Powers Act. All Americans troops except for a small military police contingent were withdrawn from Grenada by mid-December, within the sixty-day period stipulated by the act. In December, 1984, Herbert A. Blaize (born 1918), a moderate, became Prime Minister of Grenada, in the nation's first election in eight years.

H

HAIG, Alexander M. Jr. (born 1924). A career military officer acclaimed for his role in negotiating a settlement in Vietnam but sharply criticized for his involvement in the secret bombings in Cambodia, Haig rose in civilian service to become President Nixon's (born 1913) first White House Chief of Staff, and

Secretary of State under President **Ronald W. Reagan** (*see*). Born in 1924 in a suburb of Philadelphia, Pennsylvania, Haig worked at various odd jobs during his childhood, contributing to the family income after his father died when Haig was only ten years old. Haig enrolled at Notre Dame University in 1942, but left a year later to enter the United States Military Academy at West Point, securing an appointment to the academy with the assistance of a politically influential uncle. In 1947, he received a B.S. degree and a second lieutenant's commission, graduating 214th out of a class of 310. After leading a rifle platoon, Haig served for a year as an administrative assistant on the staff of General Douglas MacArthur (1880-1964) in Japan. During the first years of the Korean conflict, Haig earned three medals as an aide-de-camp, participating in the Inchon landings and seeing combat in five campaigns. During the 1950s, he rose steadily through the military ranks, winning appointments as a tank commander, a West Point tactical officer, and an exchange company officer—all in the United States—before the Army transferred him to Europe, assigning him to a tank battalion and, later, to the United States Army headquarters. Haig obtained an M.A. in international relations from Georgetown University in 1961, two years after returning to the United States. He spent three years as a staff officer at the Pentagon and then, in 1964, was appointed military assistant to Secretary of the Army Cyrus Vance (born 1917), who retained Haig as his special assistant when named Deputy Secretary of Defense later that year. From 1966 to 1967, Haig commanded an infantry batallion in Vietnam, earning the Distinguished Service Cross for heroism in battle. After gaining a promotion to the rank of colonel, Haig was appointed military adviser to Henry A. Kissinger (born 1923), National Security Adviser to the newly elected President Nixon. Haig's reputation for decisiveness, tirelessness, and bureaucratic skill served him well in his powerful but demanding position under Kissinger as liaison between the State Department and the Pentagon. After receiving a promotion to Brigadier General, Haig provided President Nixon with first-hand reports on military developments in Vietnam—including the secret 1969 bombings of North Vietnamese troops in Cambodia—and in 1970, Nixon rewarded him with a formal appointment as Deputy Assistant to the President for National Security Affairs. The new position provided Haig with more direct access to the president, allowing him to screen intelligence information and prepare presidential briefings on security issues. After heading the advance party which paved the way for President Nixon's historic visit to China in 1972, and winning another promotion to Major General, Haig engaged in "shuttle diplomacy," flying back and forth between Washington and Saigon as Nixon's principal emissary to the President of South Vietnam, Nguyen Van Thieu. Haig helped negotiate a cease-fire agreement and persuaded Thieu to sign the accord. Following a brief return to active military duty as the Army Vice-Chief of Staff in 1973, Haig accepted Nixon's request in May of that year to replace White House Chief of Staff H.R. Haldeman (born 1926), who had resigned in connection with the Watergate scandal. As Chief of Staff during Nixon's final year of office, Haig exercised much more power than most appointees to that position, while the president became more and more consumed by Watergate. Many political observers during that period, including Watergate special prosecutor Leon Jaworski (1905-1982). credit Haig with maintaining staff morale and ensuring that the executive branch continued to function at all during the months preceding Nixon's resignation. When the President, facing articles of im-

THE MACMILLAN PUBLISHING COMPANY

Alexander Haig

peachment, relinquished his office in August, 1974, Haig emerged unscarred, one of the few Nixon staffers untainted by the scandal. In the weeks that followed, Haig paved the way for the transfer of power to the succeeding president, Gerald R. Ford (born 1913). Haig left the White House just six weeks after Ford assumed office. Because Haig expressed a desire to return to active military duty, Ford named him Commander in Chief of U.S. forces in Europe. Haig took command on November 1, 1974, and six weeks later also became Supreme Allied Commander in Europe in charge of all NATO forces, a post he would hold for almost five years. While in charge of NATO forces, Haig concentrated on modernizing the alliance's conventional military forces and increasing troop readiness to offset the Soviet buildup in Eastern Europe. The difficult task of reconciling the conflicting interests of the thirteen nations in the alliance demanded the kind of diplomatic skill Haig had honed in Southeast Asia during the Nixon presidency. Although he retained his command of NATO after the election of **Jimmy Carter** (*see*) to the Presidency, Haig's adamant opposition to Carter's foreign policy, particularly

with regard to the Soviet Union, ultimately spurred him to resign his commission in 1979 and retire from the military. Following a brief stint as a political science professor at the University of Pennsylvania, Haig accepted the position of President of United Technologies Corporation— a major U.S. defense contractor—in December, 1979. A year later, President-elect Ronald Reagan named Haig as his nominee for Secretary of State. Although some of Haig's activities during the Nixon years—especially his participation in wiretappings and his involvement in the secret bombings of Cambodia—came under close scrutiny by the Senate Foreign Relations Committee, Haig won confirmation by a 15-2 margin. As Secretary of State, Haig advocated clearly defined foreign policy, free of any trace of ambiguity. Toward that end, he tried to secure all power to develop and implement foreign policy decisions within the state Department, a goal he would again propose in 1987 in criticizing the fragmentation of foreign policy-making power that helped lead to the **Iran-Contra affair** (*see*). Haig came under fire in 1981 when, immediately following an assassination attempt on President Reagan, he announced to the media, "I am in control here, in the White House." Although as the senior officer of the Cabinet, Haig did have the authority to oversee White House activities during a temporary emergency, many observers interpreted his statement as an improper assumption of authority. As Reagan's Secretary of State, Haig vehemently opposed the spread of Communism, particularly in Central America, and attributed Marxist revolutions to the influence of the Soviet Union. He also adopted a tough stance against international terrorism and advocated the development of Third World nations through private initiative and investments and free markets rather than increased economic aid. But Haig's commitment to an unambiguous foreign policy controlled solely by the State Department created tensions within the Reagan administration. In June, 1982, after infighting among Haig, Secretary of Defense Caspar Weinberger, and National Security Adviser William Clark became public knowledge, Haig resigned. Returning to the private sector, he founded a Washington, D.C., consulting firm, accepted another position at United Technologies Corporation, and wrote *Caveat: Realism, Reagan, and Foreign Policy*. After establishing a political action group, the Committee for America, in 1986, Haig (unsuccessfully) sought the Republican Presidential nomination in 1988, running on a campaign of fiscal responsibility at home and, in the wake of the Iran-Contra scandal, renewing his call for "one voice" in foreign policy. Although he never did achieve his goal of the presidency, Haig, by winning powerful offices in the White House under three Republican presidents, came as close to the office as anyone can without winning an election.

HAITI. The United States occupied Haiti for 19 years—from 1915 to 1934 (see volume 14). Under American occupation many public improvement programs were carried out, and the U.S. Marine-trained Haitian Guard proved to be the best native police force in the history of the country. By 1930, resentment of the American presence was growing, and President Herbert Hoover decided to end the occupation. On August 21, 1934, the last American Marines departed, leaving as President the anti-American, Stenio Vincent. Vincent completed three terms as President, then chose Elie Lescot as his successor. In the summer of 1946, Haitians elected their first black President since the occupation, Dumarsais Estime, who secured American funds for irrigation and land reclamation. In 1950, his resignation was announced, and General Paul Magloire was elected President. While he was in office,

the United States began more aid programs and Haiti's foreign trade increased. He refused to leave office after six years and had to be forced to give up his position. Between December, 1956, and Sepember, 1957, Haiti experienced seven short-lived governments. Then, Francois Duvalier ("Papa Doc") (1907-1971) was elected President, beginning a 28-year family reign. He changed the Haitian Constitution to appoint himself President for Life and later appointed his son to succeed him. Duvalier's authoritarian rule lasted for more than thirteen years, until his death in 1971. During that time he maintained a firm grip on the government and the military and crushed all opposition in politics and the media. So paranoid was Duvalier that at one point he ordered all the weapons in Haiti gathered into one building so he could keep a close watch on them. His ruthless edicts were backed up by his dreaded secret police, known informally as the Tontons Macoute (Creole for bogeymen). Duvalier cultivated an image of himself in keeping with the *Voudon* (Voodoo) religion—a mixture of Christian and African beliefs—practiced by many Haitians. Affecting black clothes and dark glasses, he reminded many Haitians of Baron Samedi, the Voudon god who is keeper of the tombs. Duvalier's identification with the terrifying rituals of Voudon enhanced his dictatorial authority. During the Duvalier era, United States aid to Haiti was cut and reestablished several times—restored because the Haitian vote in the Organization of American States (O.A.S.) was crucial to American interests, only to be withdrawn again in disapproval of Duvalier's abysmal human rights record. In October, 1962, aid was restored because the United States needed Haitian airfields during the Cuban missile crisis. During "Papa Doc" Duvalier's administration $126.5 million was given to Haiti in U.S. military and economic assistance. When he died

in 1971, his son Jean-Claude "Baby Doc" (born 1951) took over. Jean-Claude attempted to improve Haiti's image to encourage tourism and foreign investment. He also strove to increase American aid to the desperately poor nation. As a result, tourism increased, economic assistance from the United States went up to $4,300,000 a year and $1,000,000 worth of arms were sold to Haiti by the United States. United States–Haitian relations became more friendly than they had been in years. Jean-Claude Duvalier continued to rule until February, 1986, when he fled into exile. After that a three-man provisional government led by General Henri Namphy took power. A believer in the old Duvalier ways, Namphy promised to hold free elections, but after a brief period of optimism, an outbreak of violence at the polls in the summer of 1987 destroyed any hope for a Democratic Haiti, at least for the immediate future. Two opposition presidential candidates were killed in the fall of 1987, and violence again erupted when the national Constitution was altered to prohibit any Duvalierist from running for President for ten years. Political killings increased with little response from the Namphy junta. The election violence led the United States to suspend millions of dollars in economic assistance to Haiti. Congress declared that all aid would be withheld until Haiti held a free, Constitutional election. On January 17, 1988, Lesile F. Manigat was elected President of Haiti. Opposition leaders expressed dissatisfaction with the election results by calling a general strike on February 6, 1988, President Manigat's inauguration day.

THE HOMELESS IN AMERICA. Homelessness became common for an increasing number of Americans in the 1980s. Never before, except during the Great Depression, had so many Americans lacked a permanent place of residence. While it is impossible to cite a specific figure for the number of homeless people, estimates from the late 1980s suggest that about 1% of the population—roughly 3 million people—were considered homeless. It was impossible to define a single type of person who was homeless. The homeless included single and married men and women, teenagers, children, and even whole families. They lived on the streets, in cars, under bridges, and in the few homeless shelters. Not all homeless people were alcoholic, nor were they all drug abusers, runaways, or mentally ill. The only factor they all had in common was a lack of affordable housing. The 1982 report of the Community Service Society of New York claimed that nearly 2,500,000 Americans were losing their homes each year due to increases in rent, demolition, or renovations that caused rents to go up. In addition, the amount of money available for public housing had decreased significantly since the beginning of the Reagan administration in 1981. From 1981 to 1986, the funds allocated to the federal Department of Housing and Urban Development for construction of public housing dropped drastically. Unemployment, which rose in the recession of the early 1980s, was another factor. While the federal government tended to ignore the problem of homelessness, the American public did not. Each year Americans contributed money and volunteer labor to church-sponsored soup kitchens and shelters, local charities, and national charities such as the Coalition for the Homeless. In *Callahan* v. *Carey*, in August, 1981, a New York state court established the "right to shelter" for homeless men, a right that was later extended to homeless women and homeless families. Atlantic City, Philadelphia, Los Angeles, Washington, D.C., St. Louis, and West Virginia have also recognized the right to shelter—a crucial step in finding long-lasting solutions to the problem of homeless people.

I

IACOCCA, Lee Anthony (born 1924). Few figures in the history of the American automobile industry can match the spectacular career of master car salesman and showman, Lee Iacocca. Named president of the Ford Motor Company when he was 46, he was fired eight years later by Henry Ford II, despite having just guided the company through its two most successful years up to that time. Immediately after he was fired, however, he was hired as Chief Executive Officer of the dying Chrysler Corporation. There he led a fierce and controversial fight for the company's survival that included persuading the U.S. Congress to lend Chrysler $1.2 billion. When Iacocca managed not only to turn Chrysler into a booming success, but also to repay Washington's loan in full with interest, seven years ahead of schedule, he became the nation's newest folk hero. Shrewd, out-spoken, and tough-talking, Iacocca grew up in Allentown, Pennsylvania, the son of Italian immigrants. He graduated from Lehigh University with a B.S. in industrial engineering after only three years, during which time he maintained an "A" average. Next, he went to Princeton on a Wallace Memorial Fellowship and earned his master's degree in mechanical engineering. From there he entered the Ford Motor Company's Executive Training program in Dearborn, Michigan, but after nine months he decided not to stay in engineering: "I was eager to be where the real action was—marketing or sales." Working in sales and marketing jobs at the eastern district office, in Chester, Pennsylvania, he won recognition for the first time in 1956 with his "56 for 56" program, in which he urged people to buy new Fords by paying $56 per month. Adopted as a national sales slogan, it was credited with selling 72,000 extra cars. Iacocca began rapidly

moving up the corporate ladder. After a brief period as District Manager of Washington, D.C., he was summoned to Dearborn where he became the protege of top Ford executive Robert S. McNamara (born 1916). In 1960, he was named Vice President and General Manager of the Ford Division; in 1965, he became a director of the company; in 1970, he was President. Along the way, Iacocca was responsible for developing the Mustang, a light, sporty, inexpensive car that sold an incredible 418,812 in its first year alone and changed the thinking of the American automobile industry. His autobiography, *Iacocca*, published in 1986, was a huge bestseller. In the 1980s, while struggling to save Chrysler, Iacocca was asked by President **Ronald Reagan** (*see*) to serve as chairman of the Statue of Liberty-Ellis Island Centennial Commission. It was a fitting position for a son of immigrants whose life in the automobile industry had come to embody the American dream.

IMMIGRATION. After years of debate, Congress in 1986 passed the Immigration Reform and Control Act to address the growing number of illegal aliens living and working in the United States. In 1980 alone, more than 1,250,000 million immigrants took up residence in the United States, most of them from Latin America, the Caribbean, the Far East, and Indochina. Many entered the nation illegally; the number of illegal aliens was estimated at 3,900,000 by 1986. Beginning in 1981, a bipartisan effort to draft an immigration reform bill in Congress focused on penalizing employers who hired illegal aliens, and offering legal status to a majority of the illegal aliens already residing in the United States. A Republican-dominated Senate easily passed forms of the bill in 1982 and 1983. Faced with budget restrictions, the House could reach no accord on the issue. The final version of the bill, passed in October, 1986, includes a

A smiling Mexican woman holds the residency papers which will allow her to live and work in the United States.

special amnesty program for agricultural workers—immigrants who worked in American fields at least 90 days in each of the previous three years became eligible for temporary and then permanent status. In addition, illegal aliens residing in the United States since 1982 became eligible for legal permanent status. Employers were required to check citizenship papers, and those with a pattern of illegal hiring practices could face criminal charges. In May, 1987, thousands of immigrants came to the Immigration and Naturalization Services (I.N.S.) offices to take advantage of the new amnesty program. The I.N.S. estimated that 55% of those eligible for amnesty had come to the United States from Mexico. In the months following the signing of the Immigration Reform and Control Act, statistics showed a reduction in the number of illegal border crossings from Mexico by as much as 30%.

THE INTERMEDIATE RANGE NUCLEAR FORCES (I.N.F.) TREATY.

On December 8, 1987, United States President **Ronald Reagan** (*see*) and Soviet Secretary General **Mikhail Gorbachev** (*see*) signed a historic treaty, the result of over six years of on-and-off negotiations between the two nations. It was "the first agreement ever to eliminate an entire class of U.S. and Soviet nuclear weapons," as the President noted during the signing ceremony. According to the terms of the agreement, both nations—"*conscious* that nuclear war would have devastating consequences for all mankind" and "*convinced* that the measures set forth in this treaty will help to reduce the risk of outbreak of war and strengthen international peace and security"—agreed to destroy all U.S. and Soviet land-based nuclear missiles with a targeted range of between 500 and 5,500 kilometers (312 to 3,437 miles), including those deployed in eastern Europe's Warsaw Pact nations and the western European countries belonging to the North Atlantic Treaty Organization (N.A.T.O.). The I.N.F. talks, specifically designed to reduce the number of nuclear missiles based in Europe, had begun late in 1981. In June, 1982, the two nations had also resumed discussions aimed at reducing longer-range strategic arms (Strategic Arms Reduction Talks, or START)—despite the fact that the Senate had failed to ratify the 1979 Strategic Arms Limitation Treaty (SALT II) following the Soviet invasion of Afghanistan in December, 1979. The Soviet Union, protesting the American deployment of intermediate-range Pershing II missiles in Europe, abandoned both sets of negotiations in 1983, but on March 12, 1985, both the I.N.F. and START negotiations resumed in Geneva, Switzerland, yet both nations faced an immediate obstacle. Gorbachev insisted that any negotiations should jointly encompass three separate issues: intermediate range missiles; long-range (strategic) missiles; and research into systems designed to destroy incoming missiles and orbiting satellites. President Reagan, on the other hand, refused to consider scrapping research on his proposed anti-missile system, the Strategic Defense Initiative (S.D.I.) project, popularly called "Star Wars." He insisted that the negotiations consider the three separately. The Geneva talks accelerated after Gorbachev, proclaiming his desire for peace between the two nations and an end to the arms race, agreed to negotiate each issue separately. The treaty was signed in Washington, D.C., on December 8, 1987—the first day of the third summit meeting between the two leaders and the first U.S. visit by a Soviet leader since **Leonid Brezhnev** (*see*) had met with President Richard Nixon (born 1913) in 1973. The treaty held that "no later than three years after entry into force of this Treaty, all intermediate-range missiles of each party, launchers of such missiles and all support structures and support equipment . . . associated with such missiles and launchers, shall be eliminated." Missiles included under the agreement are U.S. Pershing II and ground-launched cruise missiles and Soviet SS-4 and SS-20 missiles. The treaty also detailed a 13-year verification program that would allow each nation to conduct as many as 20 on-site inspections per year of the other country's missile operating bases and missile-support facilities. These verification procedures applied not only to the two principal nations in the agreement, but also to two Warsaw Pact nations (East Germany and Czechoslovakia) and five N.A.T.O. members (West Germany, Belgium, Great Britain, the Netherlands, and Italy). The treaty, of "unlimited duration" once in force, requires each nation to provide six months' notice of any intention to withdraw from the treaty. Although the December, 1987, summit meeting saw limited progress in reaching accords in other areas of nuclear-arms control, the I.N.F. treaty itself represented, in Gorbachev's words, "a historic milestone in the chronicle of man's eternal quest for a world without wars."

IRAN-CONTRA AFFAIR.

The Iran-Contra Affair was perhaps the severest crisis of **Ronald Reagan**'s (*see*) presidency. The several individuals and groups who investigated the affair discovered that a small group of high-ranking administration officials had conducted a complex series of covert activities, possibly with the knowledge and approval of the President, in direct violation of the Constitution and of congressional legislation. The affair grew out of two of the Reagan administration's most cherished goals: freedom for Americans held hostage in Lebanon by pro-Iranian Islamic extremists, and continued support for the Contra forces fighting to overthrow the leftist Sandinista government in **Nicaragua** (*see*). President Reagan was an ardent supporter of military aid to the Contras. Congress, however, passed two amendments, in 1982 and 1984, forbidding the use of federal funds to finance activities intended to overthrow the government of Nicaragua. Furthermore, in 1983, Congress set a $24,000,000 ceiling on aid to the Contras. In early 1984, this money had nearly run out, and those in the administration involved in aiding the Contras—especially National Security Adviser Robert McFarlane (born 1937) and his aide Marine Corps Lieutenant Colonel Oliver L. North (born 1943)—began to seek new sources of funding. The Government of Saudi Arabia agreed to contribute $1,000,000 a month to the Contras. In March, 1984, pro-Iranian extremists seized a Central Intelligence Agency (C.I.A.) Official in Beirut, Lebanon—an incident that deeply concerned Director of Central Intelligence **William Casey** (*see*). Six other Americans were kidnapped in Beirut in 1984 and 1985. In May, 1985, an N.S.C. official met with Prime Minister Shimon Peres (born 1923) of Israel to discuss the possibility of a new American policy toward Iran. Relations between the United States and Iran had been poor, to say the least, during the Reagan administration. The long, frustrating **Iran Hostage Crisis** (*see*), the rise in Iranian-sponsored

The Ayatollah Ruhollah Khomeini.

terrorism, and the vehemently anti-American stance of Iran's Islamic fundamentalist ruler, the Ayatollah Ruhollah Khomeini (born 1900?), and his fanatical followers had produced tension and hostility between Washington and Teheran. But Iran seemed to be the key to freeing the American hostages in Lebanon. If contact could be made with "moderate" elements in the Iranian government, and an agreement reached, Iran might use its influence in Lebanon to win the hostages' freedom. Accordingly, the N.S.C. drew up a directive proposing overtures to Iran and sent it to top administration officials for review. Most were unenthusiastic, including Secretary of Defense **Caspar Weinberger** (*see*), who wrote on his copy of the directive, "This is almost too absurd to comment on." Nevertheless, the N.S.C. continued its intiative, especially after Israeli officials proposed a plan to ship American TOW missiles—potent antitank weapons— to Iran, with Israel acting as the middleman in the transaction. In July, 1985, President Reagan gave guarded approval to the sale of TOW missiles to Iran. On August 6, Mc-Farlane briefed President Reagan more fully on the N.S.C.-Israeli proposal. What transpired at that meeting is still in doubt. McFarlane would later testify that Reagan gave

his approval for the sale of American weapons to Iran. Reagan would at first say that he had, but later claimed that he simply could not recall whether he had or had not. On August 20, the first shipment of TOW missiles was sent to Iran from Israel. More followed in September, and in November, 18 HAWK anti-aircraft missiles were shipped to Iran aboard a C.I.A. aircraft. In Central America, Oliver North, aided by retired Air Force General Richard V. Secord (born 1932), set up a covert air operation to supply the Contras. On November 25, 1985, the C.I.A., which was also involved in the Contra supply operation, reported to the President that no more aid could be sent without specific top-level authorization. According to testimony from Vice Admiral John Poindexter, McFarlane's deputy and, after McFarlane's resignation in December, 1985, National Security Adviser, Reagan authorized the operation, but his order was later destroyed. By March, 1986, the Contra supply operation, operating initially from a military airfield in El Salvador, was in full swing. Early in 1986, Reagan again authorized arms shipments to Iran with the intention of cultivating relations with Iranian "moderates." The N.S.C. staff, however, was growing dissatisfied with Iran, as only one American hostage had been freed in Lebanon. N.S.C. officials, including North, later met with Israeli and Iranian officials in London, West Germany, and—in May, 1986—in Teheran itself in an effort to gain the release of all the hostages, but the Iranians demanded more and better weapons as a condition. By this time, the two seemingly unconnnected initiatives in Central America and Iran converged. North had had what he was to call a "neat idea." The arms shipments to Iran were not gifts; profits from the sales reached into the millions of dollars. Money was needed to keep the Contras fighting and the supply planes flying; North decided to divert the profits from the

Iran arms sales to the Contras, through Swiss bank accounts. On April 4, North sent Poindexter, McFarlane's successor, a memo explaining the plan. Poindexter then prepared to send it to President Reagan—which according to his later testimony, he did not do. In August, 1986, a story appeared in *The New York Times* suggesting that the N.S.C. was raising funds for the Contras. North was called before the House Intelligence Committee and denied the allegations—denials which he later testified were outright lies. But the resupply operation would not remain secret much longer. In September, Costa Rican officials disclosed that Contra-support operations were being carried out from an airstrip in that country. On October 5, one of the resupply planes was shot down over Nicaragua. The sole survivor, Eugene Hasenfus, an American, was captured and sentenced to thirty years in prison by a Nicaraguan court. He was released several months later in a good-will gesture by the Sandinista government. The Iranian operation was deteriorating as well; despite meetings with Iranian officials in Washington, D.C., and West Germany, and more arms shipments to Iran, as many hostages had been taken in Lebanon as had been released. The tangled web woven by North, McFarlane, Poindexter, and their associates now began to unravel rapidly. On November 3, 1986, a Lebanese magazine, *Al Shiraa*, reported that McFarlane had led an American delegation to Teheran and that American weapons had been shipped to Iran. The Iranian government and the American press confirmed the story, despite a denial by the White House. Congress expressed concern; shipping arms to Iran had been prohibited by the Arms Control Export Act of 1979, and President Reagan had stated, forcefully and repeatedly, that he would not deal either directly or indirectly with terrorists. Several Middle Eastern nations expressed anger; the arms shipments were a violation of the United States' declared neutrality in the Iran-Iraq war. In a press conference on November 19, President Reagan admitted that the United States had sold arms to Iran, but contended that the amount shipped to Iran was "less than a planeload" and consisted of only "defensive weapons and spare parts." Actually, Iran had received over 2,000 TOW missiles. Two days later, C.I.A. Director Casey appeared before the House and Senate Intelligence Committees to answer questions about the C.I.A.'s role in the November, 1985, arms shipment. Expressing confusion, Attorney General Edwin Meese III (born 1931) offered to conduct an inquiry. On November 25, 1986, the scandal blew wide open when the connection was revealed between the two seemingly separate affairs. Meese announced the discovery of an N.S.C. memorandum linking the arms-for-hostages deal and the covert effort to aid the Contras. Meese was criticized for his announcement; there was a time lapse before FBI agents were brought into the investigation, and Meese did not act immediately to protect vital evidence. Some even implied that Meese's investigation was itself a form of cover-up—forewarned that an investigation of N.S.C. activities was in the offing, North had had time to destroy confidential documents. With public and congressional furor growing, a special prosecutor, Lawrence M. Walsh (born 1912), was appointed, both the House and Senate set up investigating committees of their own, and President Reagan appointed a commission, chaired by Former Texas Senator John Tower (born 1924), to explore the role of the N.S.C. in the affair. The Tower Commission, as it came to be called, issued its report on February 26, 1987. It was sharply critical of President Reagan's style of management. Whether or not he had known or approved of the diversion of funds, concluded the commission, his lack of contact with his top advisers had allowed them to pursue improper and illegal intiatives. A bipartisan Congressional committee made up of 11 members of the House and Senate, chaired by Senator Daniel Inouye (born 1924), heard testimony from hundreds of witnesses between May 3 and August 5, 1987. A number of the hearings were nationally televised. To the many millions of Americans who watched the hearings, Oliver North proved the most intriguing and appealing figure of the affair. A Vietnam veteran decorated for bravery, North's work for the N.S.C. had involved him with such operations as the invasion of **Grenada** (*see*) in 1983 and the capture of the Palestinian terrorists who hijacked the cruise ship *Achille Lauro* in 1985. North promised the committee he would tell "the good, the bad, and the ugly" about his part in the affair, and his testimony at times resembled the plot summary of a suspense novel. North's candid account was peopled with a cast of characters including retired U.S. military officers, Iranian businessmen, Arab royalty, and shadowy international go-betweens. It was clear to the Committee that the covert activities of North and Poindexter had been both long-standing and widespread. North—a capable witness who sparred verbally with committee members—implied that the late William Casey had played a major role in planning the arms-for-hostages swap and the contra-aid effort. The precise truth about Casey's involvement may never be determined: He died of cancer as the hearings began. He had resigned as C.I.A. Director in February. North, trim, crew-cut, and resplendent in his medal-bedecked Marine uniform, became to many Americans as President Reagan once described him, "a national hero." He was seen as a patriotic, dedicated officer who had taken matters in his own hands to do what he perceived as his duty. But to others, he was a dangerous man, a zealot who had disregarded the law by running an illegal operation from his office in the White House basement. A major question which the committee sought to answer concerned the extent President Reagan had been involved in the affair. Had he known that the Iran initiative was originally conceived, as North asserted, as a simple arms-for-hostages swap? Had he known or approved the diversion of profits to the Contras? Some observers had predicted that the hearings would uncover a so-called "smoking gun" —a piece of evidence revealing the extent of President Reagan's knowledge and approval of the activities of North, Poindexter, and their associates. It was expected to come during Poindexter's testimony, which followed soon after North's. Poindexter—North's boss and the one man between North and the President—testified that in December, 1985, he had destroyed a document that indicated the President had approved a shipment of Hawk missiles to Iran with the knowledge they were part of an effort to free the hostages in Lebanon. But Poindexter also testified that he had intentionally withheld knowledge of the diversion of funds to the Contras from the President, thereby protecting the President. This testimony, which could be neither proved or disproved, left some skeptical: Poindexter had reduced his credibility as a witness by claiming ignorance in response to a great many of the Committee's questions. A later witness was Secretary of State **George Shultz** (*see*), who had opposed the arms sales, and angrily disapproved of the secret deciding of foreign-policy matters. He also stated that Iran had taken the United States "to the cleaners." Indeed, it had: A year after the first shipments of arms had reached Iran, only three hostages had been released—and three more had been taken. Thus, the United States had lost international prestige in the affair, Iran had gained large quantities of American arms, and the number of hostages in Leb-

anon had remained the same. While the several committees and commissions were investigating the affair, the FBI and the Grand Jury under Lawrence Walsh conducted investigations of their own with a view to returning indictments. The President did not appear before the Committee, but in a televised speech on August 12 he told the nation that his sincere desire to free the hostages and establish relations with "moderates" in the Iranian government had become unfortunately "tangled up" with the arms sale. The Iran-Contra affair did not destroy Reagan's presidency, as Watergate had Richard Nixon's, but it did severe damage. As a result of the affair, Reagan's Chief of Staff, National Security Adviser, and C.I.A. Director had resigned. And the affair led many Americans to lose faith in Reagan's leadership ability and the integrity of his administration.

THE IRAN HOSTAGE CRISIS. On Sunday, November 4, 1979, a mob of about 3,000 screaming students and other demonstrators poured over the walls of the embassy compound in Teheran, Iran, occupied the building, and seized more than 60 Americans as hostages. For the next 444 days the fate of the 53 American hostages in Iran became a major preoccupation of the American public and a source of frustration and embarrassment for the administration of President **Jimmy Carter** (*see*). The failure of Carter's diplomatic efforts to free the hostages and the disastrous collapse of an attempted military rescue mission were important factors in Carter's loss of the 1980 Presidential election to **Ronald Reagan** (*see*). The storming of the U.S. Embassy in Teheran came at a time of violent transition in Iran. Shah Mohammed Reza Pahlavi (1919-1980), the Western-oriented ruler of Iran since 1941, had become increasingly dictatorial by the 1970s, establishing a one-party state in 1975 that was propped up by SAVAK, a hated secret police

force that had free rein to arrest and torture opponents of the Shah. Underground opposition to the Shah coalesced around fanatic Moslem fundamentalists who acknowledged the exiled Ayatollah Ruhollah Khomeini (born 1900?) as their leader in both spiritual and secular matters. By late 1978, Iran was rapidly approaching a state of anarchy as young Khomeini supporters formed large processions and beat themselves with fists and chains as they marched through the streets during the intense fervor of a religious observance in December. The Shah formed a new government, but it failed to slow the revolutionary tide, and he abdicated in January, 1979, flying first to Egypt, then to Morocco, the Bahamas, and finally Mexico, where it was learned that he had an advanced case of cancer. In late October, the Shah was admitted to the United States for medical treatment, a move that triggered the seizure of the U.S. Embassy a few days later. Two weeks after the Embassy takeover, Khomeini, with great fanfare, ordered the release of women and black hostages, because "Islam has a special respect toward women, and since blacks, who have spent ages under American pressure and tyranny, may have come to Iran under pressure." Five women and eight black men were freed and flown to Wiesbaden, West Germany, but two women and one black were still held by the militant students, who claimed they were spies. With the release of the 13 hostages, U.S. authorities learned to the further embarrassment of the United States, that most of the Embassy's classified files had also fallen into the militants' hands. One more hostage, an American suffering from multiple sclerosis, was released in July, 1980. As the weeks wore on, it became obvious that diplomatic efforts to free the hostages were getting nowhere. So in late April, 1979, the United States launched a secret military strike with the goal of penetrating all the way into Teheran, capturing the Embassy, freeing the hostages, then flying out quickly from an unused airfield. The strike was in trouble shortly after it began. One of eight RH-53D helicopters launched from the U.S.S. *Nimitz* was abandoned in the desert when a warning light indicated a potential rotor-blade failure. A second helicopter turned back because of malfunctions in its flight-instrument system, and a third chopper landed at the rendezvous point with a hydraulic leak that put it out of action. All had encountered a smothering dust cloud that delayed the timetable more than an hour. The mission was aborted, but then, during refueling, a helicopter collided with a C-130 refueling aircraft, which burst into flames. Eight crew members died and five were injured. The remaining choppers were abandoned, and the survivors departed on the C130 transports. In the fall of 1980, Iran was invaded by Iraq. Hard pressed by this new development, and more inclined to deal with the Carter administration than with a new administration that after the elections might be headed by **Ronald Reagan** (*see*), Iran began negotiating in earnest in November, 1980, with Algeria serving as an intermediary. Agreement was finally reached on January 19, 1981. In broad terms, it provided for the release of approximately $8 billion in Iranian assets in the United States that had been frozen by the Carter administration in retaliation for the seizure of the hostages. The 52 hostages were released on January, 20, 1981, their 444th day of captivity, and the day **Ronald Reagan** (*see*) was sworn in as President. The hostages were flown to Wiesbaden, West Germany, where they were greeted by former President Carter on January 22.

J

JACKSON, Jesse. (born 1941). Despite his protests that he was "just a country preacher," Jackson—a candidate for the Democratic Presidential nomination in 1984 and 1988 and a protege of Dr. Martin Luther King, Jr. (1929-1968)—rose to become the predominant black leader in the United States in the 1980s. Jackson, whose ancestors included black slaves and Cherokee Indians, was born in 1941, the son of an unwed domestic worker who married a postal employee and janitor two years after Jackson's birth. After spending one year at the University of Illinois on a football scholarship, Jackson transferred to the all-black North Carolina Agricultural and Technical State College in Greensboro, where he became student body president and an honors student in sociology and economics. In 1963, while at Greensboro, Jackson became an active participant in the campus civil rights movement, organizing sit-ins and picket lines at segregated public places, restaurants, and other businesses, gaining statewide recognition for his efforts. After receiving his B.A. degree in 1964, Jackson won a scholarship to the Chicago Theological Seminary, but he left the seminary one semester short of graduation to work full-time for Dr. King's Southern Christian Leadership Conference (S.C.L.C.). Jackson's success in heading the Chicago branch of the S.C.L.C.'s Operation Breadbasket, a program that used boycotts and picketing to pressure the city government into providing better jobs and services for the black community, led to his appointment as national director of that program in 1967. The S.C.L.C. considered naming Jackson as King's replacement after King was assassinated, but instead chose the Reverend Ralph Abernathy as its new leader. After being ordained a Baptist minister in 1968, Jackson remained active in the S.C.L.C. for three more years before leaving in 1971 to found Operation P.U.S.H. (People United to Save Humanity), an organization formed to "push for a greater share of economic and political power for poor people in

Jesse Jackson

America." Jackson emphasized the importance of education and economic growth to black progress, and P.U.S.H. gained widespread attention as a national vehicle for reviving racial pride. During the Bicentennial of the Declaration of Independence, in 1976, Jackson, as President of Operation PUSH, initiated a crusading program to curtail the pervasive problems of vandalism, drug abuse, pregnancy, and high dropout rates among students attending inner-city schools, assisted by a $200,000 grant from the Ford Foundation. Calling on his formidable skills as an orator, Jackson took charge of the self-help program himself. He visited urban high schools nationwide and preached a message of hard work and high aspirations. In 1979, on a highly publicized tour of South Africa in which he advocated civil disobedience in protest against apartheid laws, Jackson began to establish himself as an international figure. Later that year, Jackson undertook a tour of the Middle East, promoting acceptance of the **Palestine Liberation Organization** (*see*). This tour prompted allegations of an anti-Israeli bias, a criticism which continued to haunt him during his Presidential campaigns in the 1980s. In 1983, Jackson took a leave of absence from P.U.S.H. to mount an ambitious voter registration drive, launching his long-shot campaign to win the Democratic Presidential nomination in 1984. Jackson formally announced his entry into the race on November 3, 1983, promising to represent "the poor and dispossessed of this nation," and to create a "rainbow coalition" of the disenfranchised: racial minorities, women, and the underprivileged. Jackson's candidacy won the support of some black leaders, but many in the black Democratic establishment, including such prominent political leaders as Andrew Young (born 1932) and Mayor Tom Bradley (born 1917) of Los Angeles, grew concerned that Jackson's campaign would divide the Democratic party and ensure President **Ronald Reagan**'s (*see*) re-election; they instead supported the candidacy of **Walter Mondale** (*see*). Jackson's campaign received a boost early in 1984, when he personally appealed to Syrian president Hafez al-Assad (born 1925) for the release of United States Navy pilot Lieutenant Robert O. Goodman, Jr., who had been held captive for over a month after his plane had been shot down over central Lebanon on December 4, 1983. Securing the freedom of Lieutenant Goodman was a diplomatic coup for Jackson, who was praised for his role by President Reagan. Campaigning relentlessly, maintaining a twenty-hour-a-day schedule despite exhaustion and occasional pain from sickle-cell anemia, Jackson delivered as many as five speeches a day throughout the primaries. He also toured Latin America that June, meeting with El Salvador's President Jose Napoleon Duarte (born 1926), Nicaragua's **Daniel Ortega** (*see*), and Cuba's Fidel Castro (born 1927). An off-handed remark in which he referred to Jews as "Hymies" and his close association with Louis Farrakhan, head of a militant Black Muslim faction, sparked charges of anti-Semitism, alienating Jackson from one of the minorities he had hoped to include in his "Rainbow

Coalition." Jackson's primary campaign, run on a minimal budget and unusual in its lack of radio or television advertising, failed to secure the Democratic nomination, as Jackson emerged with clear-cut victories only in the District of Columbia and Louisiana. Although he had won too few delegates to exercise a substantial influence on the party platform, Jackson hailed his campaign as a victory for inspiring millions of disenfranchised Americans to enter the political process by registering to vote. After the campaign, Jackson resumed his position as President of PUSH and vowed to continue the voter-registration drive that had helped his own candidacy in 1984. Jackson's political activism remained strong in 1985, as he participated in a re-enactment of the 1965 civil-rights march from Selma to Montgomery, Alabama, was arrested for demonstrating against apartheid at the South African embassy in Washington, D.C., and met with Soviet leader Mikhail Gorbachev, appealing to him on behalf of Soviet Jewry. In 1986, Jackson formally announced the establishment of his National Rainbow Coalition and unofficially opened his 1988 presidential campaign. A gifted orator who employs a powerful, inspiring voice, sweeping hand gestures, and evangelical enthusiasm, Jackson's most lasting message may lie in his encouragement of disenfranchised audiences to join him as he proclaims, "I am somebody. I may be poor, but I am somebody. I may be on welfare, but I am somebody."

POPE JOHN PAUL II (born 1920). When Cardinal Karol Wojtyla of Krakow, Poland, was chosen Pope in 1978, he became the first non-Italian leader of the Roman Catholic Church since the Dutch Pope Adrian VI in 1522. He also became the first Pope from Poland, and the first from a Communist country. His predecessor, Pope John Paul I, had died of a heart attack just 34 days after being elected. Both

Popes chose the two-part name to symbolize their dedication to the programs of the Popes who conducted the Second Vatican Council (1962-65): John XXIII (1881-1963) and Paul VI (1897-1978). Karol Wojtyla was born in Wadowice, Poland, May 18, 1920, of working-class parents. As a teenager he worked in stone quarries and a chemical factory, and studied poetry and drama part-time in Krakow. After the German invasion in World War II, he joined a clandestine theater group. In the fall of 1942 he registered in an "underground" seminary. After his ordination as a priest in 1946 he studied theology at the Pontifical Atheneum in Rome, and by 1954 he was teaching philosophy at the Catholic University of Lublin. Later he was on the faculty of the University of Krakow. From this period come most of the poems he collected and published in 1979 under the title *Easter Vigil and Other Poems*. Professor Wojtyla was named Archbishop of Krakow by Pope Paul VI in 1964 and Cardinal in 1967. Within a year of his appointment as Pope, John Paul II visited his native country. In nine days he spoke on 32 occasions. The Communist government acted with restraint, despite the huge crowds, almost beyond numbering, that poured into the public squares and parks to listen to their Pope. Pope John Paul II visited the United States in 1979 and again in 1987. On his first trip he started in Boston, then went on to New York, Philadelphia, Des Moines, Chicago, and Washington, D.C., where he celebrated a Mass on the Mall between the Capitol and the Lincoln Memorial that drew a crowd of 175,000. His second visit, in September, 1987, was a strenuous swing through the South and West, including stops at Miami, Columbia, South Carolina—in the heart of the Protestant "Bible Belt,"—New Orleans, San Antonio, Phoenix, Los Angeles, and San Francisco. He ended his trip with visits to Detroit and the heavily Polish city of Hamtramck, Michigan. The Pope then went on to Canada, where, among other things, he conducted a mass for 4,000 Indians at Fort Simpson, Northwest Territories. Throughout his tour of the United States, John Paul II reiterated the traditional position of the Catholic Church on such issues of interest to Americans as priestly celibacy, the role of women in the church, abortion, and homosexuality. In between his two trips to the United States, John Paul II was shot and wounded on May 13, 1981, by a Turkish terrorist, Mehmet Ali Agca, who was caught and later convicted.

L

LIBYA. The North African nation of Libya, for centuries a colony of Turkey and for much of the twentieth century of Italy, gained its independence in 1952. In 1969, a military coup toppled the royalist government and a new leader, the flamboyant Muammar Qaddafi (born 1942), rose to power. In the late 1970s, Libya, like Iran, grew increasingly anti-American. Qaddafi, a proponent of global Islamic revolution, praised acts of terrorism and, according to the U.S. government, allowed international terrorists to use Libyan military facilities for training. In December, 1979, a Libyan mob attacked the U.S. embassy in Tripoli, and all U.S. diplomatic personnel were withdrawn. In 1981, the Libyan embassy in Washington, D.C., was closed by order of the U.S. government, and two months later the United States broke off all relations with Libya. Most of the approximately 2,000 Americans in Libya—almost all oil-company employees—began to leave the country. In August, 1981, Soviet-made Libyan warplanes attacked U.S. Navy jets over the Mediterranean Sea off the Libyan Coast; the American planes responded by shooting down two Libyan aircraft. Tensions between America and

Libya were further heightened in December, 1981, when U.S. officials stated that "hit squads" of Libyan terrorists, ordered to assassinate President Reagan and other leaders, had infiltrated into the United States. While no "hits" occurred, security around the President—who had already survived one assassination attempt that year—was tightened. Qaddaffi further infuriated American leaders by providing sanctuary for **Palestine Liberation Organization** (*see*) personnel driven out of Lebanon by Isareli forces in 1982. In December, 1985, Qaddaffi declared that terrorist attacks on airports in Rome and Vienna, which had claimed 20 lives, were "heroic." In March, 1986, a U.S. Naval task force arrived in the Mediterranean for maneuvers and was met with an ultimatum from Qaddaffi. He declared the Gulf of Sidra—technically considered international waters—to be Libyan territorial waters and pledged to attack any American ships and planes crossing the "Line of Death"as he called the northern limit of the Gulf. On March 24, U.S. ships crossed the line, and the Libyan military fired six soviet-made missiles at the American fleet. None reached their targets, and U.S. forces sank two Libyan vessels and attacked a

missile-launch site on shore. Despite his failure to inflict any damage on the American ships, Qaddaffi hailed the attack as a "triumph."A month later, evidence was discovered that apparently linked Libya with two recent terrorist acts, an explosion aboard a TWA flight from Rome to Athens, in which four Americans died, and the bombing of a West Berlin nightclub, which killed two Americans. The United States was joined by 12 European nations in denouncing Libya as responsible for the incidents, and President Reagan ordered a military strike against Libya in retaliation. On April 14, 1986, 18 U.S. Air Force F-11 fighter-bombers left their base in England on a 12,000-mile flight to Libya. Denied the use of French or Spanish airspace, they were forced to detour around the European coast. At 2:00 a.m. on the morning of April 15 they struck five targets in and around the Libyan capital of Tripoli. At the same time, 15 Navy warplanes, launched from two American aircraft carriers, attacked the Libyan city of Benghazi. The planes inflicted considerable damage to both cities. One Air Force plane, apparently struck by Libyan anti-aircraft fire, was lost with its two crewmen. As with all of President Reagan's military ventures,

Libyan officials show journalists the wreckage of the Libyan Naval Academy in the outskirts of Tripoli. The academy was almost completely destroyed in the American air raid on Libya in April, 1986.

American public reaction to the raid was mixed. Most Americans sided with the President's decision to bomb Libya as a demonstration of the American commitment to battle terrorism, but some protested it as a useless gesture that would serve only to increase Libyan hatred of America, especially when it became known that, although Qaddaffi had escaped harm, one of his adopted children had been killed. Shortly after the raid, President Reagan, speaking on national television, stated, "Self-defense is not only our right; it is our duty. I warned that there should be no place on earth where terrorists can rest and train and practice their deadly skills. And I meant it."

M

MONDALE, Walter Frederick (born 1928). Appointed to the U.S. Senate in 1964 and twice returned by the voters of Minnesota for full terms, Mondale was **Jimmy Carter**'s (*see*) choice for Vice President on the Democratic ticket in 1976. The two standard-bearers waged a vigorous campaign that ended in a close victory over the Republican slate of President Gerald R. Ford (born 1913) and Senator **Robert J. Dole** (*see*). Four years later the Carter-Mondale team would go down to defeat at the hands of **Ronald W. Reagan** and **George Bush** (*see both*). Mondale was born on January 5, 1928, in Ceylon, Minnesota, the son of a Methodist minister. Nicknamed "Fritz" in his boyhood, Mondale graduated from the University of Minnesota in 1951 and its law school in 1956, after two years as an enlisted man in the Army. In 1955 he married Joan Adams (born 1930) of St. Paul. As a student, Mondale had been active in the reelection of Minneapolis Mayor Hubert H. Humphrey (1911-1978). In 1960, as a practicing lawyer in Minneapolis, he managed the third successful campaign for Minnesota

Governor by Orville L. Freeman (born 1918). Freeman then appointed Mondale interim State Attorney General, an office Mondale then won on his own a few months later. He was reelected Attorney General in 1962. When Minnesota Senator Hubert H. Humphrey was elected Vice President in 1964, Governor Karl F. Rolvaag (born 1913) named Mondale to fill Humphrey's unexpired term. In 1966, Minnesota voters returned Mondale to the Senate, as they did again in 1972. As a Senator, Mondale consistently held liberal views on civil rights, school integration, consumer and environmental protection, tax reform, and political campaign financing reform. As Vice President, Mondale served as a spokesman for the President's agenda among the legislators on Capitol Hill. Out of office after the 1980 elections, Mondale returned to Minneapolis to practice law again, but continued to serve the Democratic party on a committee that he formed to raise and distribute funds to candidates in the 1982 elections. Mondale won the Democratic nomination for President in 1984 and chose as his Vice Presidential candidate Representative Geraldine Ferraro (born 1935) of New York, the first woman nominated for this office by a major party. Mondale's campaign was directed at the unfairness in President Reagan's economic policies, and he pressed the need to reduce the national deficit, a task that would be impossible, Mondale said, without higher taxes. He also backed the Equal Rights Amendment (E.R.A.) and the concept of a nuclear freeze. With President Reagan's popularity cresting on the nation's economic recovery, the Republicans won every electoral vote except those of the District of Columbia and Mondale's home state of Minnesota.

N

NICARAGUA. American interest

in Nicaragua is nothing new. In the nineteenth century, Nicaragua—Central America's largest nation in terms of land—attracted the attention of American adventurers and business interests. With ports on both the Atlantic and Pacific oceans, Nicaragua provided a convenient route for gold-seekers on their way to California. In the early years of the twentieth century, it was considered as an alternative to Panama for an inter-oceanic canal. In 1909, a U.S. naval force appeared in Nicaraguan waters after two Americans were killed in a civil disturbance there. Marines landed in 1912, and a contingent of Marines was almost continuously present in Nicaragua for the next two decades. The Bryan-Chammoro Treaty of 1916, which gave the United States the option to build a canal and establish naval bases in Nicaragua, further increased America's influence in Nicaraguan affairs. In 1927, Cesar Augusto Sandino (1893-1934) began a guerrilla campaign against the U.S. Marines. The Marines were withdrawn in 1933, but by then they had trained an effective national guard under the command of General Anastasio Somoza Garcia (1896-1956). Somoza had Sandino killed and established himself as military dictator in 1934. Somoza was assassinated in 1956 and succeeded by his sons, including Anastasio Somoza Debayle (1925-1980). The Somozas were friendly to American interests and improved Nicaragua's economy, but the family ran the nation as a private preserve, growing wealthy at the expense of the people. By the late 1970s, Anastasio Somoza Debayle had to contend with widespread civil unrest and a growing leftist insurgency. Guerrillas, calling themselves "Sandinistas" after the earlier rebel leader, launched a major offensive in May, 1979. Within seven weeks the government had fallen, Somoza had fled the country, and the Sandinistas were established in the capital city of Managua. In an effort to establish friendly relations with Nicaragua, the United States immediately recognized the new government and sent quantities of aid. The Sandinistas promised to hold free elections, pursue a non-aligned foreign policy, and allow a diversity of political opinion. But, as had been the case in Cuba 20 years earlier, the reality proved quite different from what was promised. It would be five years before free elections were held (Daniel Ortega Saavedra, born 1945, a Sandinista leader, was elected President), and the Sandinistas proved far more receptive to the Soviet Union and Cuba than to the United States. In 1981, President Reagan cut off U.S. aid to Nicaragua, charging that the Sandinistas were supplying leftist rebels in El Salvador with Soviet and Cuban arms. The Sandinista government denied Reagan's accusations. In 1981 the Sandinistas, formerly the rebels, found themselves confronted with a guerrilla movement. Groups of anti-Sandinista rebels, collectively known as "Contras" (from the Spanish "against") began waging war against the government along Nicaragua's borders. The Contras actually were a loose collection of organizations with differing memberships—some comprised former members of the Somoza security forces, while others were led by former Sandinistas—but all were committed to overthrowing the Sandinista government. The Contras soon began to receive covert military aid from the United States. The United States also moved against the Sandinistas by secretly mining Nicaraguan ports, in an effort to cut off the flow of Cuban and Soviet supplies. This touched off international protest, and in May, 1984, the International Court of Justice in the Hague demanded that America cease its mining activities. The Contras found an outspoken, unwavering ally in President Reagan. He saw them as "freedom fighters" struggling to establish democracy in a strategic region, and eagerly pressed

Congress to pass legislation authorizing military aid. In 1985, Congress rejected a military aid package but approved $27,000,000 in "humanitarian" aid. In June, 1986, after the Sandinistas suspended civil liberties, Congress voted $100,000,000 in overt military aid for the Contras—a triumph for the Reagan administration's hard-line stance. In retaliation, the Nicaraguan government shut down the nation's sole opposition newspaper. The Contras proved able to hold their own against government troops, but they made scant progress towards their goal of toppling the Sandinista government. Their military effectiveness was hampered by factions within the Contra groups and constant infighting among their leaders. Critics charged the Contras with practicing terrorism against Nicaragua's civilian population and financing their war effort with profits from the sale of illegal drugs. The governments of neighboring nations, such as Costa Rica, became uneasy over the presence of Contra troops on their soil. Many observers believed that the Contras—who were presumed to number about 12,000—lacked sufficient equipment, training, and popular support to defeat government forces. Concern over covert U.S. aid to the Contras increased with the **Iran-Contra Affair** (*see*), as investigations revealed that profits from secret arms sales to Iran had been diverted to the Contras. The situation was further complicated when an American, Eugene Hasenfus, was captured by Nicaraguan troops, when a plane carrying supplies to the Contras was shot down in November, 1986. Sentenced to 30 years in prison by a Nicaraguan court, Hasenfus was pardoned at Christmas and allowed to return to the United States. In the United States, the war of words between supporters and opponents of Contra aid continued, with President Reagan still adamant in his support of the Contras. But popular support for the Contras was declining. In late 1987 hope for a

peaceful settlement of the conflict rose when Costa Rican president Oscar Arias Sanchez (born 1940) proposed a peace plan. Both Contra and Sandinista leaders nominally agreed to abide by the plan's provisions, and the Nicaraguan government showed signs of easing restrictions on internal opposition.

O

O'CONNOR, Sandra Day (born 1930). Praised by President **Ronald Reagan** (*see*) as "possessing those unique qualities of temperament, fairness, intellectual capacity, and devotion to the public good which have characterized the 101 brethren who have preceded her," O'Connor is the first woman appointed to the U.S. Supreme Court. The granddaughter of an Arizona pioneer who founded the family's Lazy B ranch 30 years before Arizona attained statehood, O'Connor was born in El Paso, Texas. After graduating from Stanford University in 1950, she received a law degree from Stanford in 1952, ranking third in her class of 102 students. Chief Justice **William H. Rehnquist** (*see*) ranked first in O'Connor's class. After leaving law school she received no offers from any private firms except as a legal

Associate Supreme Court Justice Sandra Day O'Connor

secretary. She turned to public service, accepting a position as the San Mateo (California) county deputy attorney. When her husband graduated from Stanford and took a position with the U.S. Army in Frankfurt, West Germany, O'Connor joined him as a civilian lawyer for the U.S. Army Quartermaster Corps. After returning from Germany, O'Connor established her own law firm in Phoenix, Arizona, in 1959. While raising a family in Phoenix from 1957 to 1965, O'Connor also worked part-time for local and state government advisory boards and committees, and for the Arizona Republican party. O'Connor resumed full-time work in 1965, accepting the post of assistant attorney general for the state of Arizona. In 1969, she was nominated to fill a vacant seat in the Arizona State Senate, a seat which she retained in 1972, running on the Republican ticket. After her re-election, the State Senate elected her majority leader, making her the first woman in any state to win that position. While serving in the Arizona Senate, O'Connor reinforced her standing within the conservative community by supporting bills to limit government spending and to restore the death penalty, a sentence she later imposed while serving as a judge on the Arizona State Court of Appeals. But O'Connor also advocated the revision of various state statutes that discriminated against women, and voted in favor of adopting the Equal Rights Amendment to the U.S. Constitution. In 1974, O'Connor shifted from the legislative to the judiciary, winning election to a judgeship on the Maricopa County Superior Court. In 1979, she was appointed to the Arizona Court of Appeals. In her writings and speeches, O'Connor has advocated a philosophy of judicial restraint, recommending a reduction in the caseload of federal courts and discouraging the intervention of federal courts in local and state matters. Federal courts, O'Connor believes, should

"defer to the state courts . . . on federal Constitutional questions when a *full* and *fair* adjudication has been given in the state court." This judicial philosophy, which coincided with President Reagan's "New Federalism," encouraged the President to appoint O'Connor an Associate Justice of the Supreme Court in 1981, a nomination that won unanimous approval in both houses of Congress. While serving on the Supreme Court, O'Connor has voted with Chief Justice Warren Burger (born 1907) and Chief Justice **William Rehnquist** (*see*) in 75% of the cases heard before the Court, particularly on issues regarding states' rights. Despite her generally conservative judicial philosophy, O'Connor's unique position has made her a role model for women and a symbol of women's improving social status.

O'NEILL, Thomas Phillip (born 1912). Affectionately nicknamed "Tip" (after an 1880s baseball player named James "Tip" O'Neill), O'Neill has been involved in American politics since his graduation from Boston College in 1936. Born in Cambridge, Massachusetts, the son of an Irish immigrant, Tip O'Neill served in the Massachusetts House of Representatives for ten years before being elected minority leader in 1947. One year later, he became the first Democrat in 100 years elected speaker of the Massachusetts House. After then-Congressman John F. Kennedy (1917-1963) ran for the senate, O'Neill was elected to the U.S. House of Representatives, where he supported such issues as the Economic Opportunity Act, the Civil Rights Acts of 1956, 1957, and 1958, and Medicare. Originally a supporter of President Lyndon B. Johnson's (1908-1972) Southeast Asia foreign policy, O'Neill later changed his position, co-authored legislation demanding withdrawal of American troops from Vietnam, and voted against President Richard M.

Nixon's (born 1913) veto of the War Powers Act. In 1971 Tip O'Neill became Whip (assistant leader) under Speaker Hale Boggs (1914-1972), and two years later was unanimously elected Majority Leader. O'Neill served as the Speaker of the House from his election in 1977 until his retirement in 1987.

P

PALESTINE LIBERATION ORGANIZATION (P.L.O.). Formed in 1964, The Palestine Liberation Organization (P.L.O.) is dedicated to restoring Arab rule over Israel by whatever means may be necessary—diplomatic, military, or terroristic. In 1974, the Arab League, an organization of Middle Eastern nations, recognized the P.L.O. as the official representative of the Palestinian people, and the United Nations granted the P.L.O. permanent observer status. In 1976, the P.L.O. became a regular member of the Arab League. Yasir Arafat (born 1929), leader of a relatively moderate faction, became chairman of the P.L.O. executive committee in 1968. Under Arafat the P.L.O. has engaged in an almost continuous war with Israel, running its military operations out of Jordan at first, then from Lebanon. In 1982, Israel invaded Lebanon to put an end to P.L.O. operations there. Thousands of P.L.O. guerillas, trapped in Beirut, were evacuated to Tripoli, Libya. Palestinians continued their struggle by stepping up terrorist attacks on American and other international targets with the assistance of a sympathetic Libyan government. A 1985 peace-settlement agreement between the P.L.O. and Jordan was severed by Jordan in 1986, citing the P.L.O.'s refusal to renounce terrorism as an instrument of policy.

POLITICAL ACTION COMMITTEES (P.A.C.s). A growing force in American politics, Political Action Committees (P.A.C.s) finance candidates for office on the basis of their support for specific issues. The increasing use of expensive television advertising in political campaigns has contributed to the escalating importance of P.A.C. funds. In 1976 there were about 600 P.A.C.s raising and distributing money; by 1984, there were 4,000. The P.A.C.s represent many special interests: insurance companies, defense contractors, corporations, labor unions, trade associations, and ideological groups, to name a few. In October, 1979, supporters of campaign-finance reform, opposing P.A.C.s because of the influence they give to well-financed special-interest groups, won House approval of a bill designed to reduce P.A.C. contributions to Congressional candidates, but the bill died in the Senate due to a filibuster the following year. Congressional candidates, especially incumbents, receive most of the money. In the 1981-1982 Congressional election cycle, P.A.C.s contributed over $83,000,000. Contributions rose to $104,000,000 in 1984. Between the 1984 and 1986 elections, contributions to Senators rose by over 50%. In 1986, the Federal Election Commission approved restrictions for P.A.C. money used in Presidential elections.

R

REAGAN, Ronald Wilson (born 1911). The oldest person, at 69, ever to be elected President, Ronald Reagan rode the crest of a strong conservative movement to win the election of 1980, and won again in 1984 with the largest electoral victory margin in the nation's history, 525-13. Throughout his two terms, Reagan has consistently earned higher approval ratings than any other President since poll-taking began. Although his administration was troubled by the **Iran-Contra Affair** (*see*), and many of his policies, actions, and appointments were

highly controversial, his personal popularity remained largely undiminished. Reagan was born on February 6, 1911, in Tampico, Illinois. His father, John Edward Reagan (1883-1941), was a shoe salesman. His mother, Nelle Wilson Reagan (1885-1961), was a homemaker and occasionally a clerk in retail stores in Tampico, Dixon, and other small western Illinois towns where the family lived. After high school, Reagan entered Eureka College, in Eureka, Illinois. There he played football, captained the swimming team, became president of the student body, and took part in school plays. After graduation, he worked as a sports announcer at radio station WOK in Davenport, Iowa, then took a similar job at station WHO in Des Moines. While in southern California covering the Chicago Cubs' spring training for WHO in 1937, Reagan was given a screen test which landed him a role in the movie *Love Is On the Air*, in which he played the part of a radio announcer. Over the next 27 years he performed in 50 feature films, chiefly for Warner Brothers. Often cast as a straight-shooting, likeable young man who seldom got the girl in Westerns and military films, he is best remembered for his roles as George Gipp ("the Gipper") in *Knute Rockne: All American* (1940), and as the young man whose legs are amputated in *King's Row* (1942). Reagan's first marriage, to actress Jane Wyman (born 1914), ended in divorce in 1949. They had two children: a daughter, Maureen (born 1941), and an adopted son, Michael (born 1945). In 1952, Reagan married actress Nancy Davis (born 1921). There were two children from the second marriage: Patricia (born 1952) and Ronald (born 1958). In World War II, Reagan served in the U.S. Army Air Force. Because of poor eyesight, he was assigned to a unit making training films. He was discharged with the rank of captain. On resuming his Hollywood career, Reagan became active in the Screen

Actors' Guild, which he headed from 1947 to 1952 and again from 1959 to 1960. Reagan also became president of the Motion Picture Industry Council, the public-relations arm of the film industry, serving six terms in the years between 1940 and 1960. During these years, the future Republican President was a Democrat, and he campaigned for Harry S. Truman (1884-1972) in the election of 1948. However, Reagan supported Dwight D. Eisenhower (1890-1969) in 1952 and later announced his affiliation with the Republican Party. In 1954, Reagan launched a second career as host of the "General Electric Theatre," a weekly television show sponsored by the General Electric Company. In between its weekly shows, General Electric booked Reagan into the company's plants for speeches to employees and to local chambers of commerce and service organizations. In this period Reagan honed his already considerable public-speaking talents while communicating his convictions about the value of the free-enterprise system, the dangers of over-regulation, and the threat of Communism. Reagan's speeches on behalf of the 1964 Republican Presidential nominee, Barry M. Goldwater (born 1909), gave him a national television audience for his positions. In 1966, Reagan was elected Governor of California. Upon his inauguration in January, 1967, he set about accomplishing his goals of cutting back welfare programs and reducing government spending, especially in the areas of medical service and education. He was reelected Governor in 1972. In 1976, Reagan challenged the incumbent Gerald R. Ford (born 1913) for the Republican nomination for President and came within 117 convention votes of winning. Upon Ford's defeat by **Jimmy Carter** (*see*) in November, 1976, Reagan began working for the 1980 Republican nomination. By November, 1979, he held a commanding lead over all his Republican rivals in press polls. He won the Republican nomination easily in June, 1980, and named **George Bush** (*see*), his closest rival for the nomination, as his Vice-Presidential running mate. Campaigning against **Jimmy Carter** (*see*) in 1980, Reagan capitalized on his opponent's failure to reduce inflation and bring about the return of the hostages in Iran. As President, Reagan immediately took action to stimulate the economy. His Economic Recovery Act of 1981 called for both tax and spending cuts. At the same time, Reagan pushed for a large increase in defense spending. Though inflation was reduced, a recession began in 1981, and the federal deficit shot upward. An assassination attempt on March 30, 1981, failed to slow the President's vigorous pace. Shot in the chest as he was leaving a Washington hotel after making a speech, Reagan recovered quickly and was back at the White House in less than two weeks. His assailant, John W. Hinckley, Jr. (born 1956), was later judged to be insane at the time of the shooting and placed in a mental institution. In 1982, Congress reversed itself and adopted higher taxes. But the budget continued to rise faster than tax receipts and the deficit continued to rise at a record rate, causing the public debt of the United States to exceed one trillion dollars for the first time in 1982. Meanwhile, Reagan had also turned his attention to international problems in El Salvador, **Nicaragua** (*see*), and the Middle East. The United States began supplying military assistance to the government of El Salvador, which was struggling against leftist rebel forces. In Nicaragua, the United States began providing covert aid to the "Contras," guerrilla opponents of the leftist Sandinista government that had assumed power after the fall of Somoza. Following Israel's drive into Lebanon in 1982 to force out units of the **Palestine Liberation Army (P.L.O.)** (*see*), Reagan committed a force of U.S. Marines to peacekeeping duties in Lebanon. In

October, 1983, a terrorist bombing destroyed the Marines' headquarters and killed 241 Marines. A few days later, Reagan authorized an invasion of the small Caribbean island nation of **Grenada** (*see*) to restore order and evacuate a number of American students after a violent Marxist coup. In the election year of 1984, Reagan's campaign stressed a healthy economy, lower inflation, and substantially improved American military strength. His Democratic opponent, **Walter F. Mondale** (*see*), warned of the danger of the mounting deficit and urged a tax increase to help offset it, a campaign strategy that backfired and contributed to a landslide victory for Reagan and Bush. Reagan began his second term focusing on reducing the federal budget, tax reform, and the development of the Strategic Defense Initiative, a projected "high tech" missile defense system that quickly became tagged "Star Wars." While battling a Democratic Congress over continued aid to the Nicaraguan Contras, the Reagan administration was rocked by the Iran-Contra Affair, which surfaced in November, 1986. Relations with the Soviet Union, which had cooled perceptibly in Reagan's first term, improved when **Mikhail Gorbachev** (*see*) rose to power in 1985. Reagan first met with Gorbachev briefly in Geneva in 1985. The two leaders conferred again at an inconclusive summit meeting in Reykjavik, Iceland, in October, 1986. Gorbachev came to Washington in December, 1987, and on December 8, the two men signed a treaty to limit intermediate-range nuclear missiles (*see* **INF Treaty**), an achievement that was acclaimed as a crucial, major step in reducing the risk of nuclear war.

REHNQUIST, William Hubbs (born 1924). William Rehnquist was born and raised in Milwaukee, Wisconsin. After serving for three years in the U.S. Army Air Force, he entered Stanford Universtity, gradu-

Supreme Court Chief Justice William Rehnquist

ating in 1948. He then went on to Harvard, where in 1950 he received a master's degree in political science. He returned to Stanford to study law, graduating first in his class in 1952. The same year he began work as a law clerk for U.S. Supreme Court Justice Robert H. Jackson (1892-1954). After completing his term as clerk, Rehnquist moved to Phoenix, Arizona, working as an associate in a local law firm from 1953 to 1956, and later as a partner. In 1958, Rehnquist served as a Special Prosecutor for Arizona. He became well-known among Arizona conservatives such as Barry Goldwater (born 1909) and Richard G. Kleindienst (born 1923). When Kleindienst was appointed Deputy Attorney general by President Richard Nixon (born 1913), in 1969, Rehnquist became assistant attorney general in charge of the Office of Legal Counsel. In 1971, Rehnquist was nominated for the Supreme Court by Nixon, and despite efforts by liberal Democrats in the Senate, his appointment was confirmed. As an associate justice, Rehnquist earned a reputation for doggedly standing by his beliefs, often raising the sole dissenting voice in Supreme Court decisions. He also became known for his strong conservative outlook. In 1973, Rehnquist wrote one of the two dissenting opinions in *Roe* v. *Wade* (*see* **The Right to Life/Pro-Choice Debate**), which gave women a Constitutional right to abortion. In 1979, Rehnquist opposed court-ordered busing as a means of promoting school desegregation. He also dissented from Supreme Court decisions banning prayer in public schools. Rehnquist's conservatism echoed that of President **Ronald Reagan** (*see*), and Reagan nominated him for the post of Chief Justice following the retirement of Warren Burger (born 1907). During his confirmation hearings, Rehnquist was again criticized for his stances on women's rights and civil rights, but he won Senate approval, and on September 26, 1986, he was sworn in as Chief Justice of the United States.

THE RIGHT TO LIFE/ PRO-CHOICE DEBATE.

In 1973, the United States Supreme Court guaranteed women the constitutional right to an abortion, in a 7-2 decision in the case of *Roe* v. *Wade*, a landmark decision which has been the source of bitter controversy ever since. Prior to the Court's decision, it was a criminal offense in 44 states to receive or perform an abortion. *Roe* v. *Wade* overturned these laws on the grounds that they infringed on a woman's constitutional right to privacy. After reviewing the medical and technological evidence concerning abortion, the Court defined three stages of pregnancy, each with its own legal status. During the first trimester (three months) of pregnancy, the women's right to abortion is assured; the states are allowed to regulate abortion only in the second trimester, and then only in ways that would protect the woman's health. During the third trimester, when the fetus is able to survive outside the womb, the states may prohibit abortion—except in cases where the woman's life is endangered. Far from settling the controversy over abortion, *Roe* v. *Wade* became the focal point of a passionate debate.

Since 1973, abortion has become the most common surgical procedure for women of reproductive age, and one of every four pregnancies in the United States now ends in abortion. Supporters of the *Roe* v. *Wade* decision applauded it as a victory for "reproductive freedom"—the idea that a woman has the right to control her own body. Opponents of abortion call it murder. Every January since 1974 there have been rallies in Washington and other cities, held by both pro-choice (supporting a woman's right to abortion) and right-to-life (opposing abortion) groups to mark the anniversary of *Roe* v. *Wade*. These demonstrations often turn into emotional confrontations between the opposing groups, and are a visible sign of the deep convictions underlying the debate. It is a battle of fundamental beliefs, of opposing views on morality, ethics, and the nature of life itself, and many on each side believe there can be no compromise. At its most extreme, the controversy has provoked violence; scores of abortion clinics around the nation have been bombed or attacked—acts of terrorism that are roundly condemned by mainstream right-to-life groups. Pro-choice supporters charge that such violence is the inevitable result of often inflammatory anti-abortion rhetoric, which sometimes portrays supporters of abortion rights as killers and equates the pro-choice movement with Nazism. The fight became increasingly political in the late 1970s, as parts of the right-to-life movement joined forces with the Moral Majority (*see* **Rise of the Religious Right**) to back right-to-life political candidates and press for anti-abortion legislation. In most cases, however, pro-choice organizations, enlisting the support of such groups as the National Organization for Women (N.O.W.), have succeeded in overturning such laws in court. In 1985, the right-to-life cause was aided by the release of *The Silent Scream*, a graphic film which claimed to document the actual abor-

tion of a 12-week-old fetus. The film was distributed around Capitol Hill by the National Right To Life Committee. Right-to-Life groups praised the film and its emotional impact, while pro-choice supporters claimed it was riddled with medical inaccuracies and had been heavily edited to achieve the desired effect on viewers. The controversy concerns medical science as well as morality. Advances in medical technology have made abortion in the later stages of pregnancy safer, while at the same time premature babies have survived at increasingly early ages. This dilemma has led many to question whether the original trimester framework of *Roe* v. *Wade* is still appropriate. Even if the ruling is reworked, or change in the Supreme Court membership leads to an overturning of the ruling, the abortion controversy will almost certainly continue to deeply divide the nation.

RISE OF THE RELIGIOUS RIGHT.

In the late 1970s and early 1980s, a new and vocal movement asserted itself in American politics: the so-called Religious Right. Beginning in 1980, conservative fundamentalist Christians organized by the millions to influence Presidential, as well as Congressional, and local elections. Their efforts reached a high point in the 1988 Presidential campaign, when the Reverend Pat Robertson (born 1929), a former television evangelist, spent more than $10,000,000 in his bid for the Republican nomination. In June, 1979, the Reverend Jerry Falwell (born 1933), of Lynchburg, Virginia, formed the Moral Majority, an organization intended to gather conservative Christians into a unified voting force to oppose abortion, homosexuality, pornography, and the Equal Rights Amendment. Falwell's followers advocated increased U.S. military spending, prayer in public schools, and the teaching of the Biblical theory of creation, rather than evolution, in public schools. By registering over 2,000,000 voters, the Moral Majority contributed to the defeat in 1980 of **Jimmy Carter** (*see*) as well as of several prominent liberals in Congress. **Ronald Reagan** (*see*) won the support of Christian fundamentalists during his 1980 campaign and received Falwell's endorsement for his reelection campaign in 1984. Congressional upsets influenced by the Moral Majority in 1980 prompted liberals to focus their efforts in 1984 on the Congressional elections to reduce the political influence of the Christian fundamentalist right. In 1987, the Reverend Pat Robertson, former leader of the Christian Broadcast Network, announced his bid for the Republican Presidential nomination. Robertson's victory in the Iowa caucus in 1988 demonstrated the continuing power of the Religious Right to bring in the vote in modern American Presidential politics.

S

SHULTZ, George Pratt (born 1920). A former labor mediator, George Shultz achieved his greatest success in arms limitation talks with the Soviet Union during the Reagan Administration. Shultz was born in New York City on December 13, 1920, and spent his childhood in Englewood, New Jersey. He attended private school at the Loomis Institute in Windsor, Connecticut, graduated from there in 1938, and entered Princeton University, becoming an economics major. In 1942, after graduating *cum laude* from Princeton, Shultz joined the Marine Corps. He saw action in World War II, rising to the rank of Captain. In 1945, he entered Massachusetts Institute of Technology to work on a doctorate in industrial economics. He became particularly interested in labor relations and wrote his thesis on collective bargaining in the shoe industry. He received his Ph.D. in 1949, staying on at MIT as an assistant professor. In 1953, he served on arbitration

George Shultz

panels for labor-management disputes. In 1955 he was appointed senior staff economist for the President's Council of Economic Advisors. He resigned from MIT in 1957 to become a professor at the University of Chicago Graduate School of Business, where, in 1962, he became dean. While at Chicago, Shultz also served as a labor-relations consultant to three presidents and served on the boards of several business firms. In 1968, Richard M. Nixon (born 1913) completely surprised Shultz by choosing him as Secretary of Labor. Shultz subsequently moved from Labor to the Office of Management and Budget, and became Secretary of the Treasury in 1972. He dutifully carried out wage and price controls as ordered by Nixon, although he disagreed with them, earning a reputation as a team player. When Nixon ordered him to use the Internal Revenue Service to harass his political opponents, however, Shultz refused. He survived Watergate with his integrity intact, a figure of stability in a scandal-ridden administration. In 1974, Shultz joined the Bechtel Corporation, and a year later became its president. When **Ronald Reagan** (*see*) needed a successor to **Alexander Haig** (*see*) as Secretary of State in 1982, Shultz was chosen immediately. Shultz and Reagan engineered a May, 1983, peace agree-

ment between Israel and Lebanon, sending U.S. Marines into Beirut to keep order after the withdrawal of Israeli and Syrian forces. Tragically, the Marines became the target of a terrorist bombing which claimed 241 lives. The remaining troops were withdrawn. Since the bombing, Shultz has been committed to developing more forceful responses—such as the bombing of Libya in 1986—to international terrorism. In 1985, Shultz met with Andrei Gromyko (born 1909) of the Soviet Union in Geneva, Switzerland, to discuss nuclear-arms limitations, paving the way for summit meetings between President Reagan and General Secretary Mikhail Gorbachev (born 1931) in Geneva in 1986, Iceland in 1986, and Washington, D.C., in 1987. Shultz has continued to push successfully for nuclear-arms limitations, despite persistent opposition by the Defense Department. In South Africa, Shultz's policy of "constructive engagement" gave way to harsher actions implemented by Congress. Adherence to the Reagan doctrine, which labels any Communist government a threat, resulted in American support of "Contra" guerrilla forces in Nicaragua despite substantial public disapproval. In December, 1985, Shultz threatened to resign in response to a Presidential directive that would have required high-ranking U. S. officials to submit to lie-detector tests for security reasons. The directive was substantially altered following his protest. He again threatened resignation in November, 1986, over the sale of arms to Iran in exchange for American Hostages in Lebanon. In 1987, following the **Iran-Contra Affair** (*see*) investigation, Shultz emerged, as he had after Watergate, unblemished, strengthening his reputation as one of the Reagan administration's most capable and trustworthy members.

SOUTH AFRICA/APARTHEID. South Africa has been struggling with apartheid since 1948, when the policy was created by the nation's white minority to control the non-white majority politically and economically. Although the anti-apartheid movement has gained worldwide support, the policy continues. In 1950, the Group Areas Act established separate residential and business sections of urban areas for each race. Opposition to apartheid laws was organized by the African National Congress (A.N.C.). In 1960, 69 demonstrators died at the hands of police while protesting laws restricting their freedom in designated sections. Further demonstrations followed, and the South African government retaliated by banning the A.N.C.. In 1964, ANC leader Nelson Mandela (born 1918) was jailed for life on a sabotage charge but continued to inspire anti-apartheid action. In 1970, every black, regardless of actual residence, was assigned to one of ten nominally independent homelands created in 1959. Citizens of the homelands do not possess South African citizenship and are therefore excluded from participating in the government, on which they remain economically and politically dependent. The homelands have received no international recognition. In 1976, students in Soweto, a black suburb, protested the use of Afrikaans, the principal language of the white minority, in their schools. When police moved in to break up the demonstration, a riot erupted. Throughout the rest of 1976, riots broke out in other townships as protestors demanded equal rights and an end to apartheid. Among critics of the government arrested and detained was Stephen Biko, who died, in 1977, of head wounds received while in police custody. Pieter W. Botha (born 1916), who became Prime Minister in 1978, called for limited constitutional change regarding apartheid, amending some laws and banning the word "apartheid." The policy, however, continued. Unrest continued also, and black guerrilla activity increased. Between 1977 and 1983, the ANC, operating from neighboring Angola, Zambia, and Tanzania, claimed a number of major sabotage bombings inside South Africa, indcluding a 1980 attack on a fuel complex near Johannesburg that caused $7,000,000 million in damage, and a 1983 car bombing in Pretoria that killed 18 persons. Rioting occurred in September, 1984, in black townships, with violent repression by South African security forces. In March, 1985, police killed a number of mourners at a black funeral, arousing international condemnation. In July, the government declared a state of emergency which lasted until March, 1986, resulting in almost 8,000 arrests and over 700 deaths. Nineteen eighty-six marked the tenth anniversary of the Soweto uprising; in August of 1986, 24 people were killed by security forces during a rent strike. In October, Anglican Archbishop Desmond Tutu (born 1931), a black South African, received the Nobel Peace Prize for his work opposing apartheid. Sit-ins at the South African embassy in Washington, D.C., beginning in 1984, eventually involved over 3,000 arrests and helped focus American attention on the anti-apartheid movement. In October, 1986, President **Ronald Reagan** (*see*) signed an executive order imposing economic sanctions on South Africa. By March, 1987, more than 60 U.S. companies had withdrawn from South Africa.

STOCKMAN, DAVID ALAN (born 1948). David Stockman rose to prominence as President **Ronald Reagan's** (*see*) Director of the Office of Management and Budget, and was a major proponent of "supply-side" economics, a conservative economic theory based on the idea that tax cuts could stimulate production, providing increased revenues down the line. Stockman later abandoned this theory and eventually resigned his post in protest against the rise in federal deficits that the policy had helped bring about. Stockman was born in Camp Hood, Texas, on November 10, 1948, and grew up on a farm in southwest Michigan. He worked for the Barry M. Goldwater (born 1909) campaign in 1964, the year he graduated from high school. While at Michigan State University, Stockman was a spokesman for Vietnam Summer, a campus antiwar group. He graduated cum laude in 1968 with a B.A. in American History and accepted a scholarship at the Harvard Divinity School. At Harvard, Stockman came under the influence of Daniel Patrick Moynihan (born 1927), who was both a professor of economics and Special Assistant to President Richard M. Nixon. Stockman left Harvard in 1970, without taking a degree, to become Congressman **John R. Anderson's** (*see*) Special Assistant. In 1972, Stockman became executive director of the House Republican Conference. He and Anderson eventually split ideologically, Anderson growing more liberal and Stockman increasingly economically conservative. Stockman returned to Harvard in 1974 as a fellow at the John F. Kennedy School of Government. While there, he published an article criticizing abuse of federal social programs, which gained him recognition in conservative political circles. Deciding that the time was right to run for Congress, Stockman returned to Michigan to run for Congress. Entering Congress in 1977, Stockman served on the House Administration Committee and the Interstate Foreign Commerce Committee. He voted consistently against public-welfare programs. In 1977, he voted against additional emergency public works jobs; in 1978 he rejected a proposal to establish a consumer-protection agency, and in 1979, he voted against the creation of a Department of Education. Stockman advocated—in 1977 and 1978—defense spending measures that included production of B-1 bombers. In 1980, he joined Missouri Democratic Representative Richard A. Gephardt (born 1941) in a health-care reform bill. Also in 1980, he joined Representative Jack Kemp (born 1935), a Republican from New York, in drafting a memo to President Ronald Reagan outlining an economic plan for the new Republican Administration. Reagan then named Stockman, originally considered for Secretary of Energy, as Director of the Office of Management and Budget. Stockman considered the Office of Management and Budget the "needle's eye through which all policy must pass," the ideal place to implement his theories of supply side economics. From his association with Kemp, Stockman developed a three-year tax cut proposal, combined with a plan to cut domestic spending. Together they formed the core of the new Republican Spending Policy. Large domestic spending cuts and a three-year tax reduction were approved by Congress in 1981. In November, 1981, an interview with Stockman appeared in the *Atlantic Monthly* magazine, in which Stockman expressed doubts concerning the Reagan economic plan and Stockman's own budget calculations. The interview caused such a furor on Capitol Hill that Stockman offered to resign. Although President Reagan continually referred to Stockman as being "indispensable," Stockman continued to find himself at odds with the Administration and with Congress. Instead of balancing the federal budget as had been promised, the Reagan administration ran up the largest deficit in the history of the United States. On August 1, 1985, Stockman resigned his post at the Office of Management and Budget to join an investment firm on Wall Street. The next year, Stockman came out with a book sharply criticizing the Reagan Administration for mismanagement and shortsightedness, as well as criticism of Congress and the American people for their unwillingness to accept higher taxes and lower federal spending to balance the budget.

Margaret Thatcher

T

THATCHER, Margaret Hilda (born 1925). On May 3, 1979, Thatcher—who espouses much of the same conservative political philosophy as her American counterpart, President **Ronald Reagan** (*see*)—became the first woman Prime Minister in Great Britain's history, indeed the first modern female political leader of any European country. Nicknamed "The Iron Lady" due to her tough stance toward the Soviet Union and Britain's labor unions, Thatcher has won election three times as Prime Minister. Born Margaret Roberts, in Grantham, England, she graduated from Oxford University in 1947 and worked as an industrial-research chemist until 1951. After qualifying as a lawyer in 1953, she spent several years as a barrister specializing in taxation. She was elected to the House of Commons in 1959, and served in the Ministry of Pensions from 1961 to 1964. When the Conservative (Tory) Party regained power in 1970 under Prime Minister Edward R. G. Heath (born 1916), Thatcher served as secretary of state for education and science. Four years later, the Labour party regained control of the government,

and Thatcher split with Heath. On February 11, 1975, she won election as the new Conservative Party leader. On May 3, 1979, the British general election overwhelmingly reseated the Conservatives, with Thatcher as Prime Minister. Once in power, she advocated economic policies that were similar to themes in Ronald Reagan's campaign for the U.S. Presidency a year later: tight control of the money supply and government spending; reductions in taxation and government; and encouragement of individual initiative and entrepreneurship. Although her strict monetary policies helped successfully curb inflation, British unemployment doubled within her first two years in office and peaked at almost 14% in 1985. Thatcher regained her popularity through a military victory over Argentina in the Falkland Islands 1982. Buoyed by this victory, Thatcher won reelection in June, 1983, and continued on a conservative course. In October, 1984, she survived an assassination attempt by the Irish Republican Army—which seeks to reunite Ireland by regaining control of British-ruled and largely Protestant Northern Ireland. Despite the loss of some Conservative seats in Parliament, Thatcher, in winning her third election in 1987, became the first British Prime Minister in 160 years to serve three consecutive terms in office. On January 3, 1988, Thatcher—surpassing Herbert H. Asquith's (1852-1928) term in office from 1908-1916—became the longest serving British Prime Minister in the twentieth century.

W

WALL STREET VOLATILITY. "Black Monday," October 19, 1987, occurred amid one of the most volatile periods in stock market history. Analysts may never pinpoint the exact combination of events that triggered that day's incredible plunge of 508 points on the Dow Jones Industrial Average, the biggest drop in the history of that index, but it surely signaled a climax in an overvalued and extremely sensitive market. More than $500 billion dollars in asset value was wiped out in a day. The total losses for the two-month period ending October 19th were more than $1 trillion. Most experts attributed the following factors as probable causes: technology (computerized trading with "automatic" buy and sell orders for huge blocks of stocks preprogrammed by large institutions); deep investor concern about the U.S. economy (a weakening dollar and huge trade and budget deficits); new, high-risk trading vehicles (such as index-future trading) and the broadening influence of foreign investment in U.S. Securities. Fear and greed also governed trading. Analysts feel that several of these factors converged at the same time, causing the dramatic plunge of October 19 and the days surrounding it. According to market records kept by Salomon Brothers, Inc., four of the most volatile market swings ever occurred within that one week. On October 19, the market lost 508 points, or -22.61%, and the following day, October 20, it gained 102.27 points, or 5.88%. That was followed by another gain on October 21, of 186 points, or 10.15%. Most of these gains were wiped out on October 26, by a loss of 156.83 points, or -8.04%. Exchange officials tried in vain to limit the damage by temporarily shortening trading hours and halting computerized program trading. The Federal Reserve Board moved quickly to assure major banks that the Fed would back up their support of brokerage houses— a few of which went bankrupt nonetheless. President Reagan cautioned the nation against panic, "because all the economic indicators are solid," and he attributed the plunge to profit- taking. A Presidential commission was appointed to study the causes of the collapse. A subsequent Securities and Exchange Commission report documented how devastating computer trading could be. There had been other big swings in

the stock market in recent years. When President Gerald Ford (born 1913) announced an anti-inflation plan on October 9, 1974, the Dow Jones Industrial Average (DJIA) reacted with a 28.39 point gain. A different investor reaction took place when President Carter's anti-inflation program—which did not promise any near-term relief—was announced; the market dropped 23.04 points on March 17, 1980. On September 11, 1986 the Dow Jones Industrial Average dropped 86.61 points, or -4.61%. The "Abreast of the Market" column in *The Wall Street Journal* the next day reported: "Slide was exaggerated by computerized hedging and arbitrage against stock index future; many institutional investors were selling stocks as concern rose about higher interest rates and possibly a stronger rate of inflation ahead." With technological changes such as instantaneous communication by satellite, trading now circles the globe. Money pours in and out between New York and Tokyo, Hong Kong, London, and elsewhere. Around-the-clock trading has become the norm, and stock markets a global bazaar.

WEINBERGER, Caspar Willard (born 1917). Caspar "Cap" Weinberger became Secretary of Defense on January 21, 1981, after being appointed by President **Ronald Reagan** (*see*). He was born in San Francisco, California, on August 18, 1917, and graduated from Harvard Law School in 1941. He worked in many different California state positions until, in 1970, he was appointed chairman of the Federal Trade Commission by President Richard Nixon (born 1913). At the time, he was California's Director of Finance, under Governor Ronald Reagan. He later joined the Office of Management and Budget as Deputy Director and, later, director. In 1973, he became Secretary of Health, Education, and Welfare. In 1975, he returned to San Francisco to work for the Bechtel Corporation

as vice president, director, and general counsel. As Secretary of Defense under President Reagan, Weinberger participated in the largest peacetime military build-up in the history of the United States— Almost two trillion dollars were spent for arms in the less than seven years he was in office. He approved various equipment increases for each branch of the military. The B-1 bomber, the MX missile, the "stealth bomber," and the advanced cruise missile were all approved for the Air Force. The Navy got a plan to build a 600-ship fleet, and Weinberger supported production of the Bradley Fighting Vehicle and other high-tech weapons for the Army. Military pay and benefits were also increased. Weinberger described the proposed Strategic Defense Initiative as an "astrodome that would protect the American public from the hard rain of nuclear warheads" and did his best to support the program. He received a mixed assessment from the public concerning for his ideas and accomplishments. Many Americans believed the nation has been spending too much money on the military, with defense expenditures contributing to the record federal deficits. However, Weinberger has also gained admirers for holding his his ground on many important issues. He has opposed sending United States troops abroad without public support, fearing the creation of a situation similar to the national division over American involvement in Vietnam. He was against the American presence in Lebanon during the 1980s, and he opposed the sale of arms to Iran. (*see* **Iran-Contra Affair**) Weinberger agreed with the policy of United States Navy protection for international shipping in the Persian Gulf, and supported the American intervention in Grenada. He resigned late in 1987 after six years and eight months as Secretary of Defense. His wife's health and his own concern about the direction of arms-control negotiations were cited as the principal reasons for his resignation.

INDEX

FOR ALL 18 VOLUMES

André, John, **E77**
Andros, Edmund, 102
Anglican Church, *see* Church of England
Anne, Queen (England), 126
Anthony, Susan B., **E299–300**
Antietam, 645–46
Antwerp, 14
Anza, Juan de, **E41–42**
Anzio, 1301
Apache Indians, 726, 797
Apartheid, **E663–64**
Apollo Project, 1492, 1494–1501, 1503, 1539, **E596–97**
Apple Computer, 1507
Appomattox Court House, 682, 684
Aquino, Benigno, **E633–34**
Aquino, Corazon, **E633–34**
Arab-Israeli war, 1451, 1539, 1544–45, **E615**
Arafat, Yasir, **E659**
Arbella, **E42**
Arbuthnot-Ambrister Affair, 366, **E153**
Architecture, 973–76, 1044–45
Armstrong, Neil A., 1492, 1494–99, **E597**
Arnold, Benedict, 209, 211, 216–17, **E76–77**
Aroostook War, **E189**
Arrowsmith, 1159
Art, American, 1365–83
  abstract impressionism, 1365, **E558**
  pop, 1365
Art, Indian, 26–31, 504–5
Arthur, Chester A., 878, **E337–38**
Arthur, Timothy Shay, 491, **E189**
Articles of Confederation, 254–57, 278, 282, **E78–79**
Ashley, William H., **E189–90**
Assembly line, 1509–10
Astor, John Jacob, 514, 517, **E190**
Astor Hotel, 1061
Astrolabe, **E3**
Astronautics, *see* Space flight
Atahualpa, 21, 34, **E3**
Atlanta, 678, 679–80
Atlantic cable, *see* Field, Cyrus
Atlantic Charter, **E521**
Atomic bomb, 1309, 1310, 1385, **E579–80,**
  see also Manhattan Project; Rosenberg spy case
Atomic Energy Commission, **E580–81, E583**
A.T.& T., *see* American Telephone & Telegraph
Attlee, Clement R., 1335, **E521–22**
Attu, 1298
Attucks, Crispus, **E42**
  see also Boston Massacre
Audubon, John J., **E153**
Austerlitz, 339
Austin, Moses, 518, **E189**
Austin, Stephen, 521, **E189–90**
Austria-Hungary, 1085
Austrian Succession, War of the, 131
  see also King George's War

Automobiles, 1042–43, 1057–59, 1209, 1562, **E620**
  UAW, **E582–83**
Aviators, World War I, 1116–17
Awake and Sing, 1222
Aztecs, 26–29, 34, 35, 39, **E3–4**

B

B–1, bomber, 1545
B–29, bomber, 1309–10
Babbitt, 1159
Babcock, Orville E., 707, **E262–63**
Baby M case, **E634–35**
Bacon's Rebellion, **E42–43**
Badoglio, Pietro, 1297
Bagot, Sir Charles, 365, **E153**
Bailey v. *Drexel Furniture Company,* 1132
Bainbridge, William, **E115**
Baker, Howard, **E635–36**
Baker, Newton D., 1094, **E448**
Baker, Ray Stannard, **E410**
Bakke, Allen, 1549
Balboa, Vasco de, 19, 38, **E4–5**
Baltimore, 1752 view, 140
Baltimore, Lord, 99, 105
Bancroft, George, 8, 495, **E191**
Bank closings, 1178
Bank deregulation, **E641**
Bank of the United States, 370–71
Bank of the United States, Second, 401, 402
Banking Emergency Relief Act, 1182–83
Banks, Nathaniel P., **E263**
Banneker, Benjamin, **E115**
Barbary Wars, 334, **E115–16**
Barbed wire, 770–71
Baring, Alexander, **E225–26**
Barker, Sir Ernest, 9
Barlow, Joel, **E116–17**
Barnard, Christiaan, 1513
Barnard, Henry, 495, **E191–92**
Barnum, Phineas T., 940, 942, **E192**
Barry, John, 224, **E79**
Barry, William T., **E153–54**
Barton, Clara, **E300**
Bartram, John, **E43**
Baruch, Bernard M., 1094, 1196–97, **E448–49**
Baseball, 936, 937, 940, 1149, 1150
  see also Aaron, Henry Louis; Doubleday, Abner; Robinson, Jack R.
Bataan Peninsula, 1292
Bates, Edward, 611, **E226**
Batista, Fulgencio, 1312–13, **E561**
Battle Hymn of the Republic, see
  Howe, Julia Ward
Bay of Pigs invasion, 1417–18, 1434, **E559**
Beauregard, P. G. T., 618, 637, **E226**
Beautiful and the Damned, The, 1160
Beckwourth, James P., **E192**
Beecher, Henry Ward, 557, 914–16, **E226–27**

Begin, Menachem, 1544
Belknap, William W., 707, **E263**
Bell, Alexander Graham, 818, **E338**
Bell, John, 609, **E227**
Bellamy, Edward, 826, **E374–75**
Belleau Wood, 1095
Bellow, Saul, **E636**
Bellows, George, **E449**
Benes, Eduard, 1312–13
Benét, Stephen Vincent, 621
Benjamin, Judah P., **E263–64**
Bennett, James Gordon, 909, 937, **E227**
Bennett, James Gordon, Jr., **E375**
Benton, Thomas Hart (artist), **E484**
Benton, Thomas Hart (Senator), 400, 517, **E154**
Berenson, Bernard, 980, 983–84, 988
Berg, Paul, 1513
Beria, Lavrenti P., 1370, 1392–93
Bering, Vitus, **E43**
Berkeley, John, 103, **E43**
Berkeley, Sir William, **E43**
Berle, Adolf A., Jr., 1239
  see also Brain Trust
Berlin airlift, 1362, **E559–60**
Berlin wall, 1418
Bermuda, during Civil War, 686
Bernard, Sir Francis, 158, **E43–44**
Bessemer converter, 816, 1074, 1075
Bethune, Mary McLeod, **E560**
Bevin, Ernest, 1335
Bicentennial, 1539–40, 1577–79
Biddle, Nicholas, 400–1, **E154**
Bierce, Ambrose, **E410–11**
Bierstadt, Albert, **E192–93**
Bilbo, Theodore G., **E522**
Bill of Rights, 302, 304, 1593, 1597, **E117**
Billy the Kid, **E300–1**
Bingham, George Caleb, **E154–55**
Birmingham, 1422, **E562**
Birney, James G., 493, **E193**
Bishop, Billy, 1116
Bishop, Maurice, **E645**
Bismarck, Sea, 1300
Black, Hugo L., 1258, **E484–85**
Black Friday, **E338–39**
Black Hawk War, **E193**
Black Kettle, 781, 785, **E301**
Black Muslims, **E562**
Black Tuesday, **E485**
Blackfoot Indians, 507
Blackout of 1965, **E597**
Blacks, 1450, 1453–54, 1456, 1547, 1549, 1552, 1592, **E597–98, E600–1, E613–14, E615, E616, E654–55**
  see also Busing
Blacks, 1420–24, 1433, 1435, 1550, 1453–54, 1456, 1457, 1459, 1552, 1592, **E560, E561–62, E581, E584, E597–98, E600–1, E613–14, E615, E616, E654–55**
Blaine, James G., 708, 910–13, 996, **E339**
Blair, Francis P., **E155**
Bland, Richard P., 884, **E339–40**
Bland-Allison Act, 885, **E340**

H

INF (Intermediate Nuclear Forces) treaty, 1571, 1573, **E650**
Inge, William, 1395, 1399
Ingersoll, Robert G., 916, **E387–88**
Innocents Abroad, 965
Insecticides, *see* Pesticides
Insulin, 1513
Insull, Samuel, 1128, **E465**
Integrated circuit, 1506
Intel Corporation, 1506
International Confederation of Free Trade Unions, **E558**
International Court of Justice, 1320
International Longshoremen's Association, **E558**
International Telecommunications Union, 1326
Interstate Commerce Act, **E335**
Interstate Commerce Commission, 1128
Iran, 1550–51, 1566–67, **E653**
Iran-Contra Affair, 1574, **E639–40, E650–53**
Iraq, 1566–67
Ironclad vessels, 688, 692
Iron Curtain, 1356
see also Cold War
Iroquois Indians, 125, 128
Iroquois League, **E56**
Irving, Washington, **E167–68**
Irving, Washington, home of, 922
Isabella, 18, 23, 37, 40
see also Ferdinand of Aragon
Isolationism, 313, 368, 1127, 1133, 1226, 1273
Israel, 1357, 1393, **E618**
see also Arab-Israeli war
Italy, 15, 18, 1085, *et seq.,* 1134, 1221, 1296–98, 1301
Communist influence, 1357
Ives J.M., *see* Currier and Ives
Iwo Jima, 1308, 1309
Izard, Ralph, 139
Izzie and Moe, **E465**

J

Jackson, Andrew, 7, 348, 366, 390, 391, 393–406, 519, 520, 884, **E128, E168–69**
Jackson, Helen Hunt, **E314**
Jackson, Jesse, **E654–55**
Jackson, Robert H., **E534–35**
Jackson, Thomas ("Stonewall"), 637, 642–43, 645, 654, **E280–81**
Jackson State College, 1475
Jacob, Henry, 171
James I (England), 49, 56, 57. 58, 60, 69, 73, **E19**
James II (England), 102, **E56–57**
James, Henry, 965, 979, 981, **E388**
James, Jesse, 839, **E335–36**
James, Marquis, 520
James, William, 961, **E388–89**
Jamestown, 63, 70, 74, **E20**

Japan, 18, 1029, 1032, 1134, 1226, 1265
Korea, 1386–87
World War II, 1274, 1291–95, 1298–1301, 1305–10, 1362, 1364
Jaworski, Leon, 1483
Jay, John, 274, 302, 304, 312–14, 316, 1594, **E128–29**
Jay's Treaty, 313, **E129**
Jeannette Disaster, **E314**
Jefferson, Thomas, 7, 9, 166, 190, 200–1, 247, 283, 286, 291–99, 302, 304, 307, 310, 333–38, 340–43, 447, 940, **E92–93, E129–30**
Jehovah's Witnesses, *see* Russell, Charles
Jenkins' Ear, War of, **E57**
Jenkins, Robert, 130, **E57**
Jenner, Albert, 1523, 1526
Jenney, William, 973, **E389**
Jewett, Sarah Orne, 964, 970, 973, **E389–90**
Job Corps, 1426
Jobs, Steven, 1507
Jodl, Alfred, 1305
John Paul II (Pope), **E655–56**
Johnny Appleseed, *see* Chapman, John
Johns, Jasper, 1365, 1377
Johnson, Andrew, 614, 697, 701, 704–6, 875, 1338, **E281–82**
Johnson, Eastman, **E423**
Johnson, Hugh S., 1186, **E496–97**
Johnson, John A., **E424**
Johnson, Lyndon B., 1424, 1426–27, 1433–34, 1446–47, 1450, 1452–53, 1474, **E577, E606, E610–11**
Johnson, Richard M., **E169**
Johnston, Albert Sidney, 637, 638, **E282**
Johnston, Joseph E., 642, 676, 680, **E282**
Johnstown Flood, **E315**
Jolson, Al, 1158, 1159, **E465–66**
Jones, John Paul, 224, **E93–94**
Jones, Robert T. ("Bobby"), Jr., 1175, 1211, 1212, **E497**
Jones, Thomas ap Catesby, 546, 547, **E242**
Jones, William R., **E424**
Jordan, Barbara, 1527
Jordan, Vernon, Jr., 1552
Joseph, 798–99, **E315**
Journal, New York, 998–1003
see also Hearst, W.R.
Judson, Edward Z.C., *see* Buntline, Ned
Juneau, 1341
Juno Beach, 1280, 1302

K

Kalb, Johann, **E94**
Kamikaze pilots, 1310
Kane, John, **E356**
Kansas-Nebraska Act, 556–57, **E242–43**

Karlsefni, Thorfinn, **E20**
Kearny, Stephen W., 523, 549, 568, 569, **E243**
Kearsarge, 693
Kefauver, Carey Estes, **E571–72**
Kelley, Oliver H., 853, **E356**
Kellogg, Frank B., **E497**
Kellogg-Briand Pact, 1134, 1211, 1213, **E466**
Kelly, Ellsworth, 1376
Kelly, Gene, 1403
Kendall, Amos, **E169**
Kennedy, Edward M., **E612**
Kennedy, Jacqueline, 1438
Kennedy, John F., 1415–18, 1422–24, 1429–38, 1494, **E559, E572–74, E581, E627–68**
Kennedy, Joseph P., **E497–98**
Kennedy, Robert F., 1454, 1456, **E612–13**
Kensington Stone, **E20–21**
Kent State riot, 1475, **E614**
Kesselring, Albert, 1297, 1301
Key, Francis Scott, 330, 348, **E130**
Khomeini, Ayatollah Ruhollah, 1551, **E653**
Khrushchev, Nikita, 1392, 1417–18, 1434, 1473, **E591–92, E637**
King George's War, 109, **E57**
King, MacKenzie, 1312–13
King, Martin Luther, Jr., 1422, 1423, 1454–55, **E562, E600, E613–14, E654**
King, Richard, **E316**
King, Rufus, 285, 338, **E130**
King Philip's War, **E57–58**
King William's War, 109, 126, **E58**
Kinkaid, Thomas, 1307–8, **E535**
Kintpuash, *see* Captain Jack
Kirkland, Lane, **E558**
Kissinger, Henry, 1474, 1479, 1482–83, 1539, **E614–15**
Kitchen cabinet, 394
Kittson, Norman, **E316**
Kleindienst, Richard, 1481, 1519
Kline, Franz, 1365, 1375
Knights of Labor, **E356**
Know-Nothing Party, 887, **E243**
Knox, Frank, 1244, 1274, **E498**
Knox, Henry, 304, **E94**
Knox, Philander, 1034–35, **E424–25**
Korea, 1320, 1386
Korean War, 1386–90, **E565, E574–75**
Kosciusko, Thaddeus, **E94**
Kosygin, Aleksei, 1408, 1409, 1450
Krimmel, John, **E169**
Ku Klux Klan, 707, 887, 1156, 1157, 1258, **E282–83**
Kunstler, William, **E600**
Kurile Islands, 1333
Kurita, Takeo, 1307–9
Kurusu, Saburo, 1273, 1274
Kwajalein, 1301

S

Tennessee Valley Authority (TVA), 1184, 1185–86, 1248
Tenochtitlán, 29, 31, **E34–35**
Tenskwatawa, **E145**
Tenure of Office Act, 705, **E293**
Tereshkova, Valentina V., 1487
Terrorism, 1565–66
Tesla, Nikola, 821, **E368**
Tet offensive, 1451–53, 1468, **E625–26**
Texas, 38, 83, 84, 561, 701, 705–6
  under Mexico, 518–19
  annexed, 520–21
  in Mexican War, 545–49
Thailand, 1537
Thanksgiving Day Feast, 80–81
Thatcher, Margaret, **E665**
Theater, 1395, 1399
  see also Musicals
Thieu, Nguyen Van, see Nguyen Van Thieu
Third World, 1544
  see also specific countries
Thirteenth Amendment, **E293**
Thirty Years War, 63, 80
This Side of Paradise, 1160
Thomas, George, 637, 672, 680, 684, **E293–94**
Thomas, Jesse, 376, **E182**
Thoreau, Henry David, 495, **E218**
Three-Mile Island, 1515, 1542, **E603**
Three Soldiers, 1160
Thumb, Lavinia and Tom, 942
Thurber, Charles, **E183**
Thurmond, Strom, 1364
Tibbets, Paul, 1310
Tibet, 1554
Tilden, Samuel J., 708, **E294**
Tilton, Theodore, **E401**
Timber and Stone Act of 1878, 846
Timber Culture Act, 773–74, **E331**
Tinian, 1306
Tippecanoe, 340–41
Titan II, 1489
Titanic, **E440**
Titov, Gherman, 1486
Tobacco, 21, 72, 75, 147, **E35**
Tobacco Road, 1222
Tocqueville, Alexis de, 250, **E183**
Tojo, Hideki, 1274, 1334, **E549**
Tokyo, 1362
Tom Sawyer, 964, 966
Tom Thumb (steam engine), 387
Tompkins, Daniel D., **E145**
Tonatiuh, 29
Toombs, Robert A., 609, 618, **E253–54**
Toscanelli, Paolo, **E35**
Townes, Charles, 1511
Townsend, Francis E., 1219–20, **E513**
Townshend, Charles, 158, 161
Townshend Acts, 164–65, **E69**
Toxic waste, 1515, 1549
Trade, colonial, 12, 14, 18, 20, 40, 66, 67, 140–41
Trafalgar, 339
Trail of Tears, see Cherokees

Transcendentalism, 495, **E218–19**
Transplants, 1513–14
Transportation, 276, 383, 407–21, 428–41, 831–43, 1129
  Act of 1920, 1128
  see also specific modes
Travis, William B., **E254**
Treatise of Artillery, 232
Treaty of Aix-la-Chapelle, see King George's War
Treaty of Fort Laramie, 526, **E219**
Treaty of Guadalupe Hidalgo, **E254**
Treaty of Morfontaine, see Convention of 1800
Treaty of Paris, 281, 312, 335, 365, 455, **E107**
Treaty of San Ildefonso, 335
  see also Charles IV
Treaty of Utrecht, **E69–70**
Treaty of Versailles, **E475–76**
Treaty of Washington, **E331**
Trenchard, Hugh, 1115
Trent, William, 132
Trent Affair, **E294**
Triana, Rodrigo de, 11
Triangle Fire, **E440–41**
Triangular Trade, **E70**
Tribune, New York, 937
Triple A Plowed Under, 1222
Triple Alliance, 1085
Triple Entente, 1085
Tripolitan War, see Barbary Wars
Trist, Nicholas, **E254–55**
Truman, Harry S., 1310, 1335, 1337–38, 1357–60, 1363–64, 1387–89, 1420, **E549–51, E559, E563, E564, E567, E575, E590–91**
Truman Doctrine, 1360, **E591**
Trumbo, Dalton, **E569–70**
Trumbull, John (painter), **E107**
Trumbull, John (poet), **E146**
Trumbull, Lyman, 612, **E255**
Truth, Sojourner, **E255**
Trusts, 826
Tubman, Harriet, **E255–56**
Tugwell, Rexford G., 1239
  see also Brain Trust
Tunney, Gene, 1150, **E476–77**
Turkey, 1357, 1360
Turner, Frederick Jackson, 374, 391, 776, 995, **E332**
Turner, Nat, 586, **E256**
Tuscarora War, **E70–71**
Twain, Mark, 905, 964–66, 967, 970, **E401–2**
Tweed, William Marcy, 913–14, **E402–3**
Twelfth Amendment, **E183**
Twentieth Amendment, **E513–14**
Twenty-first Amendment, **E514**
Twenty-second Amendment, **E591**
Twenty-sixth Amendment, 1477–78, **E626**
Tydings, Millard E., 1249, **E514–15, E576**
Tyler, John, 520–21, **E219**

U

U-boats, 1088, 89, 1092
Ubico Castañeda, Jorge, 1312–13
Uncle Tom's Cabin, 555
  see also Stowe, Harriet Beecher
Underground railroad, 554, **E256–57**
Unemployment, 1177–78, 1182, 1357
UNESCO, 1326
UNICEF, 1325
Uniforms, Revolutionary War, 235–37, 239, 240–41
Union Army, see Civil War
Unions, labor, see Labor unions
United Automobile Workers, 1224, **E582–83**
United Mine Workers, **E575–76**
United Nations, 1311–31, 1333, 1387, 1478, **E560–61, E574–75**
United States, 319, 323
United States, first map of, 277
United States Temperance Union, see American Temperance Union
UNIVAC computer, 1505
University of California at Berkeley, 1449
Upshur, Abel, **E219–20**
Urey, Harold C., 1212, **E551**
U.S.A., 1160
USSR, see Russia
Utah Beach, 1282
Utrecht, Treaty of, 128
U–2 incident, 1417, **E566, E591–92**

V

Vaca de Castro, Cristobal, **E35**
Valentino, Rudolph, 1148, 1149, **E477**
Vallandigham, Clement, **E294–95**
Vallejo, Mariano, 522
Valley Forge, **E108**
Van Buren, Martin, 394, 402, 403, 520, 550, **E183–84**
Van Buren, William, 1514
Vance, Cyrus, 1544
Vandenberg, Arthur H., 1244, **E515**
Vanderbilt, Cornelius, 862, **E368–69**
Vanderbilt, William H., 862, 863, **E369**
Vanderbilt, William K., 906
Van Devanter, Willis, 1254, 1255, 1257–58, **E515–16**
Van Druten, John, 1399
Vane, Sir Henry, **E71**
Van Rensselaer, Kiliaen, **E35**
Vanzetti, see Sacco-Vanzetti case
Vaqueros, 742–43
Vassall, William, 174, 176, **E71**
Vatican II, **E626**
Veblen, Thorstein, 1167
Venezuela, 26, 1026
Venezuela Boundary Dispute, **E441**
Venezuela Claims, **E441**
Venice, 12
Veracruz, 37

The editors of the updated edition of the *American Heritage Illustrated History of the United States* are particularly grateful for the assistance of the following individuals and institutions in the editorial development of the new volumes.

Cynthia Crippen, Felice Levy, AEIOU Inc.; American Telephone & Telegraph Company; Jeanne Bristol, Henry Burr, Gene Lane, Wendy James, Americomp; Apple Computer; Avnet, Inc.; Bantam Books; British Information Services; The Brooklyn Public Library; The George Bush for President Campaign Committee; Martin I. Elze, The Jimmy Carter Library; Harold Nash, David Napell, Pascal Perri, Robert H. Rosen, Lynn Sherinski, Shelley Wayne, Choice Publishing, Inc.; Ann Hughes, Christies; Jay Price, Commission on the Bicentennial of the United States Constitution; Jerry Johnson, Department of Defense; The District of Columbia Public Library; The Robert Dole for President Campaign Committee; Martin M. Teasley, The Dwight D. Eisenhower Library; Eleanora Schoenebaum, Facts-On-File Publishing Co.; Richard L. Holzhausen, The Gerald R. Ford Library; Kim Adler, The Ford Motor Company; Katherine M. Hopper, the Hirschhorn Museum and Sculpture Garden/Smithsonian Institution; Jessie O. Kempter, I.B.M.; The International Ladies' Garment Workers Union; E. Philip Scott, The Lyndon B. Johnson Library; James M. Cedrone, The John F. Kennedy Library; The Library of Congress; Judy Wheeler, Lockheed Corporation; Movie Star News; Peter Humphrey, N.A.S.A.; The National Baseball Library; The New York Coalition for the Homeless; The New York Historical Society; The New York Public Library; The National Archives; The National Portrait Gallery; James Hastings, The Nixon Project; The Polaroid Corporation; Frank Thomas, U.S. Postal Service; James Hintz, Kim Storbakken, Judith Welling, R. R. Donnelley & Sons Co.; The U.S. Surgeon General's Office; The United States Supreme Court; Tone Graphics; The U.S. Department of Transportation; Benedict K. Sobrist, The Harry S. Truman Library; The United Nations; Elizabeth Ingoldsby, United Technology; Kit Melick and Frank Topper, *The Wall Street Journal;* Nat Andriani, Wide World Photos; The White House; Gao Xuega, Xinhua News Agency.

Richard Eastman, Whitney Ellsworth, Scott Ferguson, Gertrude Arlene Goldberg, Anne Hardgrove, Lorna Harris, Judy Knipe, Donald Kobler, Barbara Marks, Robyn O'Connor, Kevin Osborn, Peter Pettus, Elizabeth Prince, William Schwartz, David Scott, John Shanks, Betsy Smith, Sunny Sit, Sally Vagliano, Evelyn Vogel, Charles Wills, Ellen Wilson.